1

JUDITH KNEEN

ENGLISH NOW

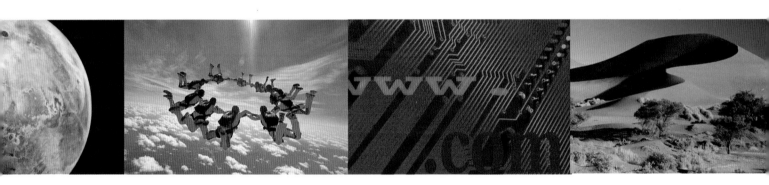

OXFORD
UNIVERSITY PRESS

Contents

WARNING:

This book will improve your English skills!

This book will make you think!

This book is fun!

Introduction

English Now will help you to improve your basic English skills *and* be a great read.

English Now 1 is split into 10 units. Each unit looks at a different topic, e.g. Fantasy worlds, Crime, Humour, Fashion. As you dip into different units, you'll find yourself laughing at daft jokes, imagining you are an alien, squirming at the horrors of the Black Death and much, much more.

Every unit has its own contents, telling you what's inside. You'll find lots of information, pictures and activities. Each unit finishes with a fun challenge, full of puzzles and brain-teasers.

Look out for these features:

- At the top of each spread you can see what you are going to learn.
- At the bottom of each spread there are smileys to help you assess what you have learned.
- Help panels give you extra ideas.

These symbols show what skills you need:

 reading

 writing

 speaking and listening

Now, all you need to do is dive in and enjoy!

Judith Kneen

3

Space

Contents

Introduction

Space is amazing. It is huge and strange. It is beautiful and dangerous.

In this unit you will use your English skills to explore space. You will:

- look at facts and figures about the Solar System
- discover incredible planets, stars and comets
- work out some alien riddles
- send messages into space
- find out about travelling in space
- design your own space suit
- learn about the dangers of space.

Finally, you will use all your English skills to do the Space challenge.

Text to share

President Nixon talks to the first men on the moon:
'Hello Neil and Buzz. I'm talking to you by telephone from the Oval Room at the White House. And this certainly has to be the most historic telephone call ever made.

I just can't tell you how proud we all are of what you have done. For every American this has to be the proudest day of our lives and for people all over the world. Because of what you have done the heavens have become a part of man's world.'

The Solar System

Understanding information texts
Writing about facts and figures

Read about the Solar System on these pages.

There are nine main planets in the Solar System. All the planets orbit the Sun. Mercury is the closest planet to the Sun. Pluto is the furthest planet from the Sun.

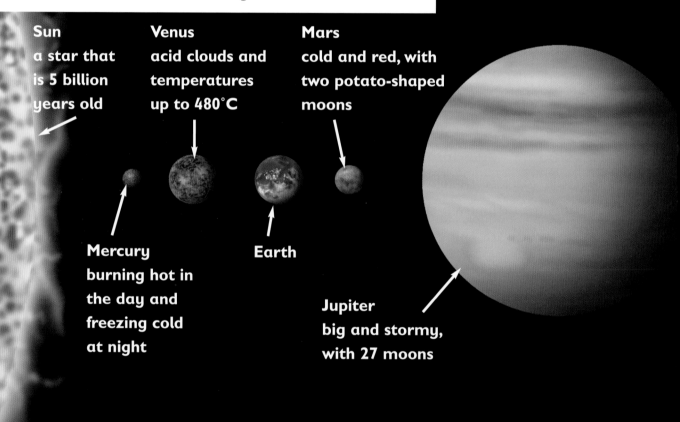

Sun
a star that is 5 billion years old

Venus
acid clouds and temperatures up to 480°C

Mars
cold and red, with two potato-shaped moons

Mercury
burning hot in the day and freezing cold at night

Earth

Jupiter
big and stormy, with 27 moons

Activities

1. What is a planet? (Use the glossary to help you.)
2. Which planet interests you most? Why?
3. What three **facts** have you learnt about the Solar System?

> **HELP**
> A **fact** is something true. It can be proved.

Glossary

methane – a gas that burns easily
orbit – move around
Solar System – the Sun and the planets that move around it

Saturn
fast spinning, with
rings of ice and rock

Uranus
blue-green colour and
covered in methane

Pluto
smallest and
coldest planet,
with one moon

Neptune
stormy with winds over
2000 km per hour

4. Write a **caption** for Earth. You could write about
   one or two of these things:
   - colour
   - water
   - land
   - moon
   - weather
   - life on Earth.
5. Choose a planet. Write two **sentences** about it. (Use
   the caption to help you.)

HELP
A **caption** describes a
picture.

HELP
A **sentence** starts
with a capital letter
and ends with a full
stop.

Stars, comets, and black holes

Read about galaxies, comets and exploding stars.

A galaxy is a big group of stars. Our galaxy is the Milky Way. It is made up of billions of stars.

A comet is made of rock, ice and gases. Its tail can be millions of kilometres long. Comets are very old.

A supernova is an exploding star.

 **Activities**

1. Read these **adjectives**. Talk about what they mean.

   - violent
   - blazing
   - giant
   - glowing
   - powerful
   - swirling
   - spiralling
   - vast

HELP

An **adjective** describes a noun (a naming word).
e.g. *a red bus*

2. Choose one of these adjectives to describe each picture on page 8. Write a sentence about it, using the adjective.

HELP

You could start your sentence:
This picture shows…

3. Read the words in the picture. They are being pulled into a black hole.

marble

empty

light

escape

collapse

Black holes are very strange.

In black holes, gravity is very strong. If you go too close to a black hole you will spiral down into it. You would never _____.

Black holes draw things into them. They are never _____.

You cannot see a black hole. This is because not even _____ can escape.

If the Earth became a black hole, it would become the size of a small _____. But it would still weigh the same as it does now.

Some black holes are made when huge stars die. They _____ inwards.

4. Use these words to fill in the text about black holes.

Glossary

gravity – a force that pulls objects towards something big, like a planet

Is anybody out there?

 Is there life on other planets? Some scientists think so.

A space craft, called *Voyager*, travels through space. It carries a golden disk. On the disk are messages – for aliens! The messages are sights and sounds from Earth.

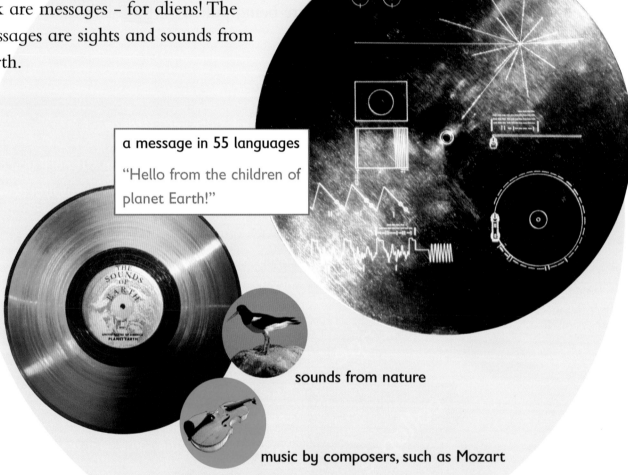

a message in 55 languages

"Hello from the children of planet Earth!"

sounds from nature

music by composers, such as Mozart

Activities

1. Imagine you can send your own disk into space.
   - Write a friendly **message** to aliens.
   - List three sounds to put on it.
   - Choose three pictures to put on it.

2. Talk about your ideas with the rest of the group. Explain your choices.

> **HELP**
> A **message** should be short and simple. Start with a greeting.

Alien riddles

3. If an alien came to Earth, what might it find puzzling? Think of three things.

4. A poet imagined he was an alien visiting Earth. He wrote a poem which described some ordinary things. Read the extracts below.

A

a room with a lock inside –
a key is turned to free the world for movement

B

But _____ is tied to the wrist
Or kept in a box, ticking with impatience.

C

At night when all the colours die,
They hide in pairs and read about themselves –
In colour, with their eyelids shut.

5. Match up the pictures to the right descriptions.

6. Write your own riddle. Describe an ordinary thing, but do not use its name.

7. Swap your riddle with a partner. Work out the answers.

HELP

Example: *They are long fingers filled with coloured blood. They bleed on flat white squares.* (pens)

1: SPACE

People in space

 Read the Fact File about people in space.

FACT FILE

- Yuri Gagarin was the first person in space.
- Neil Armstrong was the first person on the Moon.
- Helen Sharman was the first British person in space.

The Space Shuttle was the first reusable manned spacecraft. More than 600 crew have flown on the Shuttle. It usually has between five and seven people on board.

The main parts of a Space Shuttle are:
- the orbiter (this is for the crew and the cargo)
- three main engines
- two rocket boosters
- the fuel tank (the largest part of the shuttle).

Activities

1. How would you label the picture of the Space Shuttle?
2. Write an encyclopedia entry about people in space.

HELP
- Choose the information you want to use.
- Write five sentences.
- Decide on a heading and at least one picture.

Living in space

Astronauts need spacesuits for:

- protection (from radiation and changes in air pressure)
- keeping cool
- providing oxygen and water.

Spacesuits also have communication units and devices to help astronauts move around outside the spacecraft.

SPACE

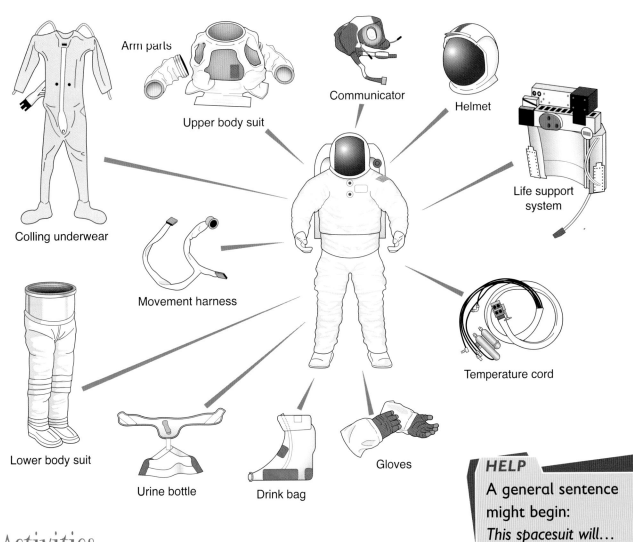

Arm parts

Upper body suit

Communicator

Helmet

Life support system

Colling underwear

Movement harness

Temperature cord

Lower body suit

Urine bottle

Drink bag

Gloves

HELP

A general sentence might begin:
This spacesuit will…

Activities

3. Design and label your own spacesuit. Include three special features.
4. Write one sentence describing your spacesuit in general.
5. Write three sentences explaining how the special features work.

HELP

An explanation might begin:
This feature is important because it…

Disasters

Sometimes things go wrong in space. In 1970, Apollo 13 was on a mission to the Moon. Suddenly, there was an explosion in the spacecraft…

A film was made of what happened. Here is part of a script.

> Jack and Jim are astronauts on Apollo 13.
> Andy is part of Mission Control at Houston, USA.
> Andy is talking to the astronauts on the radio.

ANDY: This is Houston here. We have some checks
       for you to do.

JACK: Okay, Houston.

ANDY: The oxygen tanks need checking.

(There is the sound of an explosion.)

JIM: What was that?

JACK: I don't know.

JIM: Houston, we have a problem.

Activities

1. The last words are now famous. What might Jim have been thinking when he said them?
2. Try out different ways of saying these words, to show different feelings.
3. Decide how you, as an actor, would say them. Explain your choice.

HELP
The feelings might be:
- panic
- frustration
- curiosity
- worry.

14

This is what happens next, in the film:

- The astronauts, and Houston, talk about what the problem is.
- Through a window, Jack sees gas leaking out of the spaceship.
- Jim says it must be oxygen leaking out.
- The crew have to move quickly to a safer part of the spacecraft.

Apollo 13 had many more problems. In the end, the crew came home safely.

Not all space missions end well.

Apollo 1 (1967)
Three astronauts were killed on the launch pad.

Soyuz 1 (1967)
Soyuz 11 (1971)
Three men were killed as their spaceships came back to Earth.

Challenger (1986)
All seven crew were killed in an explosion.

Columbia (2003)
Seven astronauts were killed when the Shuttle broke up

Activities

4. Write the next part of the script for Jim, Jack and Andy. Make it exciting!
5. Space is a dangerous place, but thousands of people apply to be an astronaut. Why do you think this is?

HELP
Lay out your script carefully, using:
- character names
- colons
- direct speech.

Space challenge

Complete the Space challenge. Start at number 1 and work through to number 4. Good luck!

Here are some planets. Write them out in alphabetical order.

Mercury	Venus	Earth	Mars	Jupiter	Saturn

Remember, each name starts with a capital letter.

Some products, such as sweets and newspapers, are named after things in space.

a. List three products that are named after things in space.

b. Describe each product with an adjective and a noun.

HELP
Remember each product name starts with a capital letter. e.g.
A Mars is a <u>chocolate</u> <u>bar</u>.

adjective   noun

3

A supernova is a star of great brightness – greater than normal.
The prefix 'super' can mean greater or beyond normal.

Read the descriptions below. They all have a word missing, which begins with 'super'. Fill in the missing words.

a. A large shop for buying food and other goods is called a super_____.
b. A powerful country, like the USA, is called a super_____.
c. Story characters with special powers are called super_____.

Can you think of more words starting with 'super'?

HELP

Some words beginning with 'super':
    superpower
    superheroes
    supermarket

4

Some of the punctuation from this script has been pulled away by the gravity of the planet. Copy the script, putting the punctuation back into place.

SAM: Quick! We don't have much time
ANDY What can I do?
SAM: Shut down the engine.
ANDY: When
SAM: (shouting) Now

HELP

. a full stop marks the end of a sentence
! an exclamation mark shows surprise or emotion
? a question mark shows a question
: a colon introduces something

Well done!
You have completed the Space challenge.

Natural disasters

Contents

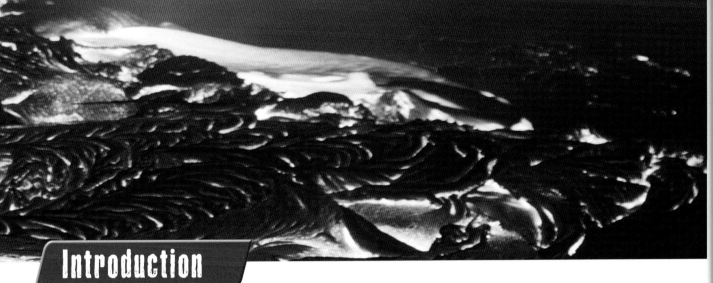

Introduction

Nature has powerful forces – forces to do with earth, fire, water and wind. They are so strong that they can cause terrible disasters.

In this unit, you will use your English skills to explore:

- where earthquakes happen
- the inside of a volcano
- the terror of a tsunami
- the power of a tornado
- how to survive a flood.

Finally, you will use all your English skills to do the Natural disasters challenge.

Text to share

Did you know?

- On average, an **earthquake** strikes the UK every four days.
- 10% of the world's population lives under threat from the 1,511 active **volcanoes**.
- Colossal **tsunami waves** travel across oceans at speeds of up to 500 mph (800 kmph).
- **Droughts** starve the land of nourishment, replacing it with mineral salts.

Earth

 Look at this map of the world. It shows the main earthquake and volcano areas.

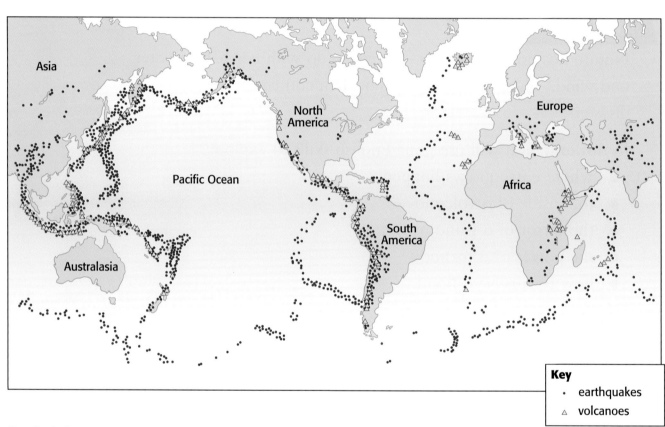

Asia

North America

Europe

Pacific Ocean

Africa

South America

Australasia

Key
- • earthquakes
- △ volcanoes

Activities

1. With a partner, make **notes** on what the map tells you about earthquakes.
   Try to make at least two main points.

2. Share your ideas with others. Use the map as evidence.

3. Agree on one **fact**. Write it in a sentence.

HELP
Notes can be just key words. You do not have to write full sentences.

HELP
A **fact** is something that is true. Evidence shows that a fact is true.

Here is some information about earthquakes. It is written for an information book.

An earthquake is a violent shaking of the Earth's surface. It happens when huge underground rocks crack together. Earthquakes take place in certain parts of the world. They tend to happen in the same places as volcanoes. The main earthquake and volcano area is around the Pacific Ocean. This area is known as the Ring of Fire. Earthquakes happen in lines or strings. This is because the Earth's surface is made up of pieces. These pieces are called plates. The earthquakes take place along the edges of the plates.

HELP

Split the text into three **paragraphs**:
- what an earthquake is
- where they happen and how they are linked to volcanoes
- the patterns of earthquakes and plates.

Activity

4. Before this text can go in the book, it must be put into **paragraphs**. This is your job.

Fire

This diagram shows the eruption (bursting) of a volcano. The labels explain what happens.

Dust rises into the sky.

Gas comes out.

Red-hot lava (melted rock) flows out.

Ash mixes with water to make mud.

HELP

A **complex sentence** has two clauses (parts). Each clause has its own verb (doing word).

Activities

1. Use the information above to finish these **complex sentences**:
    - When _____, it can block out sunlight.
    - A river of mud flows when _____.
    - _____ which smells of rotten eggs!
    - _____ which becomes hard when it cools.

2. Look at the photo of the volcano erupting. Which of the words below do you think best describe it?

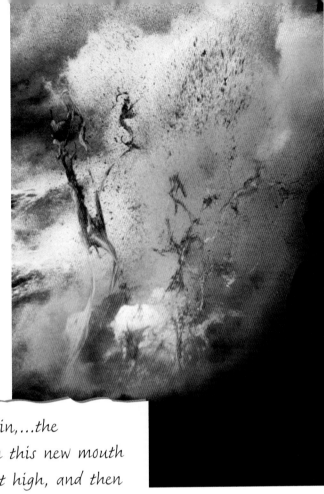

glowing   smooth   light

thick   heavy   warm

strong   menacing

In 1767, a man called William Hamilton saw a volcano erupt. It was Mount Vesuvius in Italy. He described what he saw.

> I heard a violent noise within the mountain,…the mountain split and with much noise, from this new mouth a fountain of liquid fire shot up many feet high, and then like a torrent, rolled on directly towards us. The earth shook…pumice stones fell thick upon us;…clouds of black smoke and ashes caused almost a total darkness.

Glossary

torrent – rushing stream
pumice stone – rock from a volcano

Activities

3. Good writers use words to make images (pictures) in our minds. Choosing the right words is important. Here are some comments on the writer's word choice. Copy and complete the comments.

He writes about the mountain's 'new mouth'. This suggests that the mountain is…

'A fountain of liquid fire' gives a picture of…

'Pumice stones fell thick upon us' gives an idea of…

4. The 'new mouth' is a metaphor for the open top of the volcano. Think of a **metaphor** for a flow of lava.

HELP

A **metaphor** describes something as something else. The two things need to be similar in some way, e.g. in how they look, sound, move or feel.

Water

- Finding information in diagrams

- Writing questions and headlines

A tsunami (say *soo-nar-mee*) is a huge wave. It can be made by an earthquake under the sea.

Look carefully at these two diagrams. They give information about tsunamis.

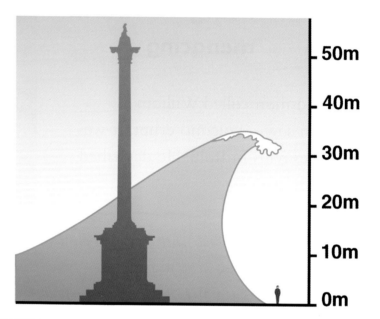

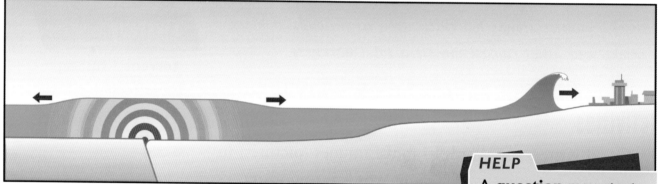

Activities

1. Write two **questions** for a partner about tsunamis.

2. Test your questions on a partner. Tell them to look at the diagrams to help them answer.

3. Try to improve your questions.

HELP

A **question** may start with words such as *how, why, where, when, what.* A question always ends with a question mark.

HELP

You may be able to improve your questions by:
- making them clearer
- choosing better words
- asking for more detail.

24

The Indian Ocean tsunami

On 26 December 2004, a tsunami hit countries around the Indian Ocean. It killed over 300,000 people.

Here are some newspaper **headlines** from just after the tsunami.

Out of the blue, a deadly wall of water

Millions lack food and shelter

'Please help. Give us aid'

Tourists return after holiday nightmare

Smashed hotel reveals its dead

Boy, two, found by aunt on the Internet

One mother's choice...which child to save

From *The Guardian* and *The Observer* newspapers

HELP

Headlines grab attention with:
* drama
* emotion
* amazing facts
* powerful quotations.

HELP

Your **headline** may include words such as *shocking, powerful, wave, buildings, flattened, crushed.*

Activities

4. What do the **headlines** tell us about this disaster? Jot down five points.
5. Which headlines grab your attention most? Why?
6. Write your own headline to go with the photo.

Wind

 The wind is a powerful force. It is full of action. Read this poem about the wind.

Glossary

buffeting – hitting or knocking

reckless – ignoring danger

I am the Wind

I am the wind
Running a reckless race
Through the town and countryside,
Through the air across the fields,
Over the ocean, beside rivers,
Blowing clouds across the sun's face,
Buffeting birds flying home.
I fight the trees, pulling away their covering of leaves,
Stealing hats and filling the sails of a sailing yacht.
I am the wind running a reckless race
Against myself.

by Julia Pearson

HELP

Verbs are 'doing' words, e.g. running, blowing.

Activities

1. List the actions of the wind in this poem. You will need to pick out the **verbs**.

2. How does the writer make the wind seem like a person?

3. What sort of character does the writer give the wind, e.g. friendly, fierce, mischievous? Think of a word to describe it and explain your choice.

HELP

When writers make things seem like people, it is called **personification**. They make them move, look or sound like people.

Tornadoes

A tornado is a very strong wind. It spins around very fast, sucking up everything in its path. It is sometimes known as a whirlwind or twister.

Here is a description of a tornado.

Glossary

Arkansas – a state in the USA

Cats and dogs have had fur ripped from their bodies, horses have had their harnesses torn away, chickens have literally been plucked alive by tornadoes.

Human victims overtaken together have been carried for miles in separate directions…A three-year-old girl was picked up in Fort Smith, Arkansas and set down unharmed three miles away.

From an article by Tim Radford, *The Guardian*, May 5 1999

HELP
Here are some words and phrases that you could use in your poem:
  a swirling rope of air
  huge
  monster
  whirling wind
  terrifying
  spiralling path
  amazing
  beast roar

Activity

4. Write a poem like 'I am the wind' but start it with:

I am a tornado…

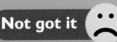

Flood

 Nowadays, scientists have ways of measuring earth movements and weather patterns. Sometimes (but not always) they can predict natural disasters and give people warning.

Imagine there has been a flood warning. You are part of a team that has been asked to make a leaflet, giving people advice.

Your leaflet needs to advise on what to do:
- before the flood
- during the flood
- after the flood.

Activities

1. With your group, discuss problems that people may face.

2. Read the tips on this page.

3. Make notes on what advice you want to give.

4. Sketch out a leaflet, including a heading. Divide it into three sections: before, during and after a flood.

HELP

Your advice should be clear and simple:

- use bullet points
- underline important things
- give firm instructions where necessary, e.g. *Go to…, Prepare…, Move…*
- offer ideas for different situations, e.g. *If…you may find it helpful…, You could…, You might want…*
- reassure people – you don't want anyone to panic!

Tip box 1
Before a flood

Homes can prepare emergency kits. This could include a torch, water and food. What else might be useful?

Move valuable things upstairs.

Tip box 2
During a flood

Move to higher ground if you can. Trying to walk or drive through flood waters may lead to injury, or loss of life. What might happen?

Tip box 3
After a flood

Help injured or trapped people. How can you do this?
Check for damage and danger in your home. What could this be?

Natural disasters challenge

Complete the Natural disasters challenge. Start at number 1 and work through to number 4.

Good luck!

1 Hurricanes are strong winds that start out at sea. They are given names to make it easier to track them.

Here are some of the names for hurricanes in 2006. They are used in alphabetical order. Put them into the right order.

Chris

Patty

Tony

Debby

Nadine

Alberto

2 Some words that end in o make the plural by adding es. Finish these words, by adding the missing letter.

v_lcanoes   po_atoes

_omatoes   tor_adoes

h_roes   e_ hoes

3 **Personification** gives human qualities to an object. It can bring writing to life.

Pick out examples of personification in the description below. Be ready to explain the examples.

The water creeps slowly up the bank. It hates land. It wants to smother all the land it can see. Water is the ruler of this planet. Air, fire and earth are just weaklings. Water will win in the end.

4 Many words describe winds:

breeze   gale

tornado   hurricane

squall   gust

Choose two of these words. Use each one in a sentence to show you know the exact meaning. (You may wish to use a dictionary.)

Well done!
You have completed the Natural disasters challenge.

The Internet

Contents

Introduction

The Internet is your link to the rest of the world. How well do you know it?

In this unit, you will use your English skills to explore:

- what makes good and bad website design
- the special words we use on the Internet
- the right and wrong ways of using e-mail
- the dangers of viruses and hacking
- some exciting stories about computers.

Finally, you will use all your English skills to complete the Internet challenge.

Text to share

> There are three kinds of death in this world. There's heart death, there's brain death, and there's being off the Net.
> Guy Almes

> The Net is a waste of time, and that's exactly what's right about it.
> William Gibson

The World Wide Web

The world wide web (www) is like a big library of websites. Anyone can make a website and put it on the world wide web.

Websites are organized into pages. Each page has the same sort of features.

This web page is from The Wildlife Trust website.

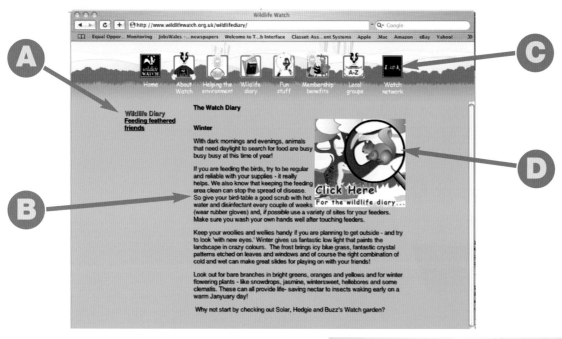

Navigation bar – pictures and words that link to other pages on the website.

Links to other web pages or websites. They are often underlined.

Text set out in paragraphs

Graphics to add colour and interest

HELP

Features that appear on some (not all) web pages:
- e-mail addresses
- headings
- page designers
- directions
- animations.

Activities

1. The labels below explain some key features on the web page. Decide which go with A, B, C and D.

2. Write two more labels to explain more **features** on this web page.

Good and bad web pages

Imagine you have asked a designer to create a web page. It is for sports centre.

This is what he has given you, but you are not happy with it.

You have noted some bad design features.

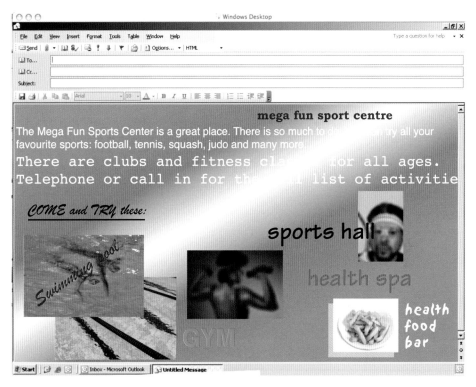

Bad design features

- heading too small and off centre
- main text – font too small, lines too long
- blue text on yellow panel is tricky to read
- too many pictures and not good choices
- need to bullet list of facilities.

Activities

3. Write a **list** of the changes you would like the designer to make.
4. Draw a rough layout of your new web page. Use labels to explain what goes where.

HELP

Divide your **list** into three parts:
- text
- background
- pictures.

Use bullets to list your points.

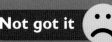

The net

The Internet is a huge communication network. It connects people all over the world, using computers, telephone lines and satellites.

Here are some reasons that we use the Internet:

To find things out

To chat to people online

To do business

To write to people, sending text and pictures

Glossary

abbreviations – short forms of words, e.g. using just initial letters

We use lots of abbreviations when using the Internet. These save time and space.

Activities

1. Talk about two more reasons why we use the Internet.

2. In the grid are some common abbreviations and their meanings. Copy the grid and fill in the middle column.

HELP

Choose from:
- Internet service provider
- world wide web
- school
- frequently asked questions
- electronic mail.

Abbreviation	Words in full	Meaning
www		The websites on the Internet
E-mail		A way of sending messages over the Internet
.sch		Part of an address that an educational place might use
ISP		The company that allows you to link on to the Internet
FAQ		Questions that are often asked, and their answers

Internet maze

When you use the Internet, you use a lot of technology. It all happens very fast.

Below is an Internet maze. Trace a path through the maze. Follow what happens when you go on the Internet to look at a web page on a computer in the USA.

1. Start at your computer.
2. The modem on your computer connects to a telephone line.
3. Your telephone line carries a message to your ISP.
4. Your ISP lets you on the Internet.
5. A satellite sends your message.
6. Your message reaches the computer in the USA.

Glossary

modem – a device that links a computer a telephone line

satellite – a spacecraft that gets and sends information

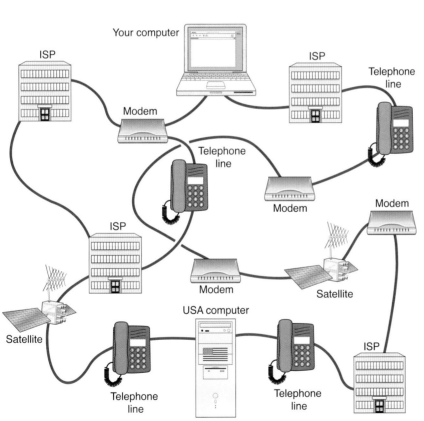

Activity

3. When the computer in the USA gets your message, it sends the web pages back to you. List the path back, starting from the USA computer and finishing at your computer.

Talking on the net

Here are some facts about e-mail.

> You can send pictures and text by e-mail.

> E-mails are cheap to send.

> Anyone can send you an e-mail.

> E-mails are easy to store.

> E-mails are quick to send.

> Anyone can read your e-mails.

> You can read e-mails when your computer is on and connected to your ISP.

It is easy to send one e-mail to lots of people at the same time. Many people get chain e-mails like the one below.

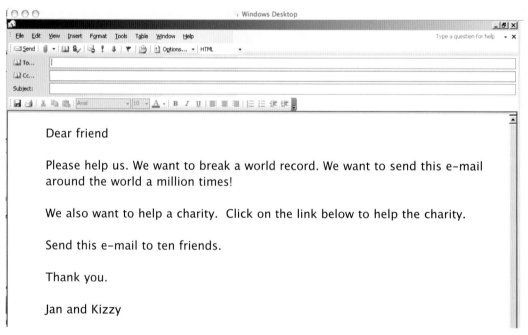

Dear friend

Please help us. We want to break a world record. We want to send this e-mail around the world a million times!

We also want to help a charity. Click on the link below to help the charity.

Send this e-mail to ten friends.

Thank you.

Jan and Kizzy

Activities

1. Divide the facts about e-mail into good and bad points.
2. Add one more point to each of your lists.
3. What would you do if you got a chain e-mail like the one above?

HELP

What questions does the chain e-mail make you ask?

Netiquette

Chat rooms let you talk online to people all over the world. It is exciting, but can also be dangerous. It is important to follow some rules for safety and good manners.

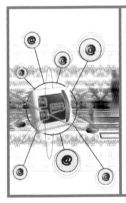

Rules for safety and good manners
1. Do not give out personal information, such as your address or telephone number.
2. Do not swear.
3. Do not use capital letters – this is like shouting.
4. Do not agree to meet people who you talk with on the Internet.

Activities

4. Which **rules** are for safety and which are for good manners?
5. Discuss some other rules for safety and good manners to add to the list.
6. Write them down.

HELP

Rules are instructions. They often start with imperative verbs, which tell you what you must do or not do.

Viruses and hackers

A virus is a computer program that harms data on computers. It can copy and spread itself to other computers. Making a computer virus is not illegal. Spreading it on the Internet is.

Here is some data on a computer, which has got a virus.

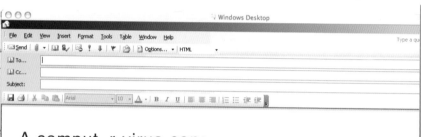

A comput_r virus can:

- L_t oth_rs hav_ acc_ss to your comput_r
- S_nd its_lf to your _mail addr_ss book
- Chang_ data on your comput_r
- Clos_ your anti-virus program.

Activities

1. The virus in the message has taken out a **vowel**. Which vowel is it?

2. Copy and complete the message.

3. Some viruses are spread by e-mail. They often use these **subject lines**:
   - I love you
   - Re: error
   - WARNING
   - Important

   Why do the virus makers use these subject lines?
   What effect do they have on the reader?

HELP

There are five **vowels** in the alphabet: a e i o u. The other letters are called consonants.

HELP

Subject lines appear in an inbox list. They tell you what the email is about.

Hacking

Hacking means breaking into someone else's computer.

Read these two views about computer hackers.

What they do is wrong.

Hackers can steal information from important organizations.

They can hack into banks and steal money.

Hackers can harm important services – like hospitals.

They are criminals.

Hackers are clever at what they do.

Hackers can be helpful. They let businesses know the weaknesses in their computer system.

Hackers do not harm anyone.

They just do it for fun.

HELP

Setting: one pupil finds another hacking into the Headteacher's computer.

Activity

4. Use the views above for a short role play. Practise with a partner, then perform in front of the group.

Cyber stories

Computers and the Internet are in many stories and films. Here are some extracts from stories that feature computers.

1

Hi! ...my mum makes things...And her latest wonder is VIMS, which stands for Virtual Interactive Mobile System. This is the story of Mum's latest miracle – VIMS – and how it almost got me killed.

From *Dangerous Reality* by Malorie Blackman

2

I carried the computer up to my room...I suppose it was kind of my dad to think of me...but I didn't like it...I had a nasty feeling that the empty dark-green glass monitor...well, I almost felt that it was staring back.

From 'Light Moves' in *Killer Camera* by Anthony Horowitz

3

Dad's worked out a way of linking hundreds of computers, all over the world. And they'll really think – like a human brain! It'll be the biggest brain in the world.

From *The Demon Headmaster Takes Over* by Gillian Cross

 HELP

A **blurb** is a short description on the back of a book.

Activity

1. Read the **blurbs** on the next page. Match them up to the right extracts.

Blurbs

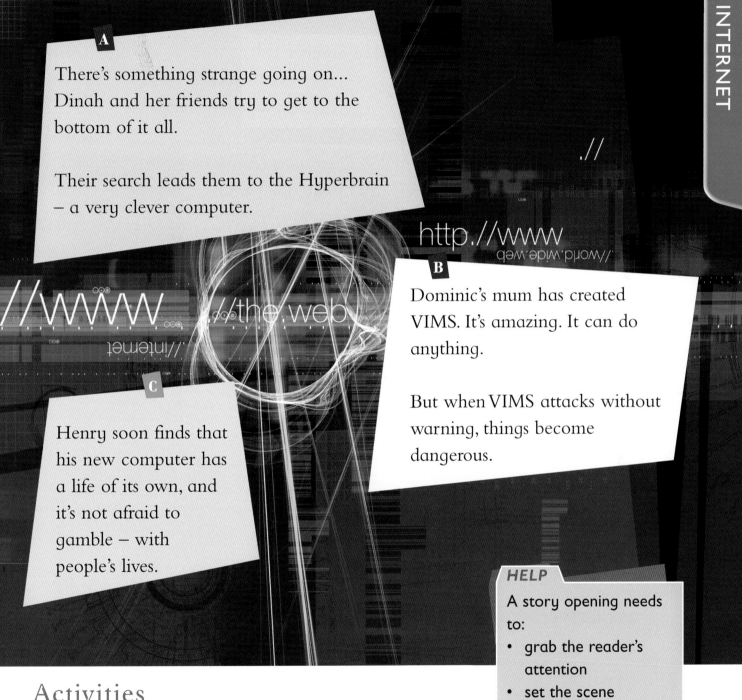

A

There's something strange going on...
Dinah and her friends try to get to the
bottom of it all.

Their search leads them to the Hyperbrain
– a very clever computer.

B

Dominic's mum has created
VIMS. It's amazing. It can do
anything.

But when VIMS attacks without
warning, things become
dangerous.

C

Henry soon finds that
his new computer has
a life of its own, and
it's not afraid to
gamble – with
people's lives.

HELP

A story opening needs
to:
*   grab the reader's
    attention
*   set the scene
*   introduce the main
    characters
*   start the plot and
    action.

Activities

2. What do the stories have in common?
3. Which story would you like to read? Why?
4. Choose one story extract. Write the next three
    sentences for it.

 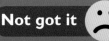

Internet challenge

Complete the Internet challenge. Start at number 1
and work through to number 4.
Good luck!

1 New words have been made to describe things on the
Internet. Some have been made from joining old words.

Join up these words and stems to make four words
about the Internet.

e	site
on	load
down	line
web	mail

1. _____

2. _____

3. _____

4. _____

2 Imperatives are commands at the start of a
sentence. They tell you what to do.

They are used for instructions or advice.

Put imperatives in these sentences.

- _____ your computer.

- _____ suspicious emails.

- _____ an anti-virus program.

- _____ copies of important files.

Do not open

Keep

Protect

Use

3 Punctuation helps the reader to read a text properly. It can help to make a story exciting and interesting.

A full stop (.) marks the end of a sentence. Short sentences can have a strong effect.

An exclamation mark (!) shows surprise or strong feeling.

A dash (–) is an informal way of adding more to a sentence. It suggests a pause.

A question mark (?) marks a question, even if the writer does not expect a response.

Put some punctuation into the start of this story.

> Hi I'm Charlie I should not be telling you this I am a computer hacker   Don't tell anyone will you I'm brilliant but I'm in danger

4 Nouns (naming words) can be dull on their own. Noun phrases make the nouns more interesting.

For example:

the monitor → noun

the empty dark-green glass monitor → noun phrase

Make these nouns more interesting by making them noun phrases.

1. He held the **box**.
2. She looked at the **e-mail**.
3. I had an **idea**.

Well done!
You have completed the Internet challenge.

Extreme sports

Contents

Introduction

Some sports are wild and risky. These are extreme sports.

In this unit you will use your English skills to:

- explore the world of extreme sports
- look at safety, fitness and skills needed in these sports
- imagine the thrills of a bungee jump
- look at extreme sport lifestyle and fashions
- read some exciting stories.

Finally, you will use all your English skills to do the Extreme sports challenge.

Text to share

Why do they do it? People who dive from the sky attached to a thick elastic band. Or battle with white water in a flimsy boat. Or climb to the top of the world where their bodies start to die. Are they mad and reckless, or daring and brave?

They play at the extremes of sport – the extremes of what the planet has to offer and the limit of what their bodies allow. But why invite such danger into life? To them it's simple, and life is at the heart of it. As someone once said: 'All who live, die. But not all who die have lived.'

Action sport

Extreme sports are getting more and more popular. Some are old sports. Others are new.

Most extreme sports:

- need a lot of skill
- can be dangerous
- are done alone, not in teams
- are done in extreme places or at extreme speeds.

Activities

1. Match the names of extreme sports with the right pictures on this page.

   snowboarding   paragliding   white-water rafting

   rock climbing   extreme cycling

2. Which of these sports are new? Which do you think have grown from old sports?

3. Write a description of 'extreme sport' to put in a **dictionary**.

HELP

Follow the style of this **dictionary** entry:

sport *noun* (*plural* **sports**)

a sport is a game that exercises your body, especially a game played out of doors

---

Young people and extreme sports

Here is a graph. It shows the extreme sports done by some young people.

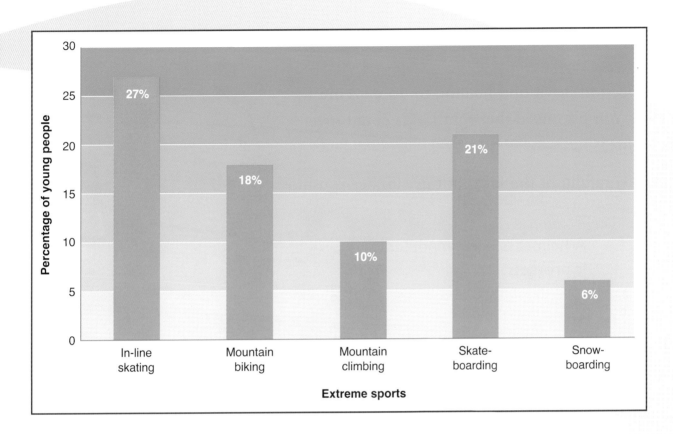

Activities

4. Look carefully at the graph. Which sport is most popular?

5. Which is least popular? Why do you think this is?

6. This graph was done in 2003. What might have changed since then?

7. 10% of young people do mountain climbing. What is another way of saying 10%? Is it:

a) $\dfrac{5}{10}$
b) $\dfrac{1}{10}$
c) $\dfrac{10}{10}$

> **HELP**
> 10% = 10 out of every 100, or 1 out of every 10.

Be prepared

You need to be fit and healthy to do extreme sports. You also need the right kit. It could save your life.

Look carefully at the kit that this climber is using.

A helmet is very important. It protects…

An ice axe will help you…

Crampons (spikes) on your boots help you to…

Ropes are fixed to the ice. They will save you if you…

Activities

1. Imagine you are the ice climber above. Copy and complete each sentence to get to the top.

2. You need to be strong and flexible to be a climber. Which parts of the body do you think need to be particularly strong?

HELP

Think about:
- the joints as well as the muscles
- small and large parts of the body.

Practice and training

To be good at an extreme sport, you need to practise and train. This helps your body to get fit and strong. It also helps you to improve your skills.

Many extreme sports need good balance. You can improve your balance with practice.

As with every sport, you have to learn the basics first.

Activities

3. Which other extreme sports need a good sense of balance?

4. Look carefully at the photo above. What skills will this young skater need to learn? E.g. balance, how to stop and turn, concentration.

5. Here are some basic **instructions** on how to skateboard. Put them in the right order.

HELP

Remember that **instruction** texts

- may use **time adverbs**, e.g. *first, next, then, last*
- may use **imperatives** (commands), e.g. *put, use, place*
- give a **sequence** of steps to follow.

Once you are going, put the back foot on the board.

Put your back foot down again to stop.

First, put one foot at the front of the board.

Use your other foot to push along.

The rush

Describing a bungee jump

Writing a poem about a dramatic moment

 Why do people do extreme sports? Lots of people do these sports for the adrenalin (say *a-dren-a-lin*) rush. This means that they get a big thrill and a buzz of excitement. Perhaps our normal lives are too quiet and safe nowadays.

Look at this picture of a bungee jumper.

Activities

 1. The bungee jumper above has just jumped. What words could describe him?

happy	scared	daring	expert	fit
worried	foolish	skilled	brave	silly

 2. Write two sentences to describe this bungee jumper. Use some of the words above.

HELP

You could use some of these sentences starters:

I think this man looks...

To do a bungee jump, you have to be...

I don't think this man is...

Extreme poetry

This photo shows the same bungee jumper, nearer the ground. He took this picture himself. (On the photo opposite, you can see his camera.)

Activities

3. Look carefully at the man's expression. Describe how he might be feeling.

4. Imagine you are the man. Put his feelings and thoughts into a short poem.
   You could start with the line 'Oh no, I just remembered…'

HELP

Here are some poetic devices you could use:

- **alliteration** (words begin with the same sound), e.g. *silent scream*
- **rhyme** (words with similar endings), e.g. *never/ever, rush/crush, dare/care.*
- **onomatopoeia** (sound words), e.g. *whiz, ping, snap, crash*
- **one word lines** – these can have great impact.

Lifestyle

Considering different views on sport

Writing a persuasive letter

Read this script with a partner.

Mal: Snowboarding is a great sport. It's fast and scary.

Jaz: Give me football any day. That's a proper sport.

Mal: Snowboarding is exciting.

Jaz: In football you play in a team. You learn skills and play other teams. It's good fun.

Mal: With snowboarding, you test yourself. You take risks and get better.

Jaz: Snowboarding is just about image. And it's dangerous.

Activities

1. Do you agree most with Mal or Jaz? Why?
2. Imagine your PE teacher wants to teach an extreme sport. Write a letter to persuade your PE teacher either to either go ahead with the idea, or to drop it.

HELP

A persuasive text may:
- **list** points to support an argument
- use **repetition**
- appeal to the reader's **emotion**
- use **rhetorical questions** (which don't need an answer)
- **exaggerate** for effect.

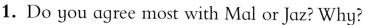

Fashion and adverts

Extreme sports have their own fashions. Sometimes these fashions become everyday clothing.

Extreme sports also have their own slang (informal words), e.g. 'wipe-out' means falling off a surf board, 'an ollie' is a skateboard jump.

Extreme sports use slogans like these:

Activities

3. List the fashions linked to skateboarding. Think about style of trousers, shoes, etc.

4. Find two more slang words linked to surfing or skateboarding. You may need to ask friends, or do some research on the Internet.

5. Look at the slogans on the t-shirts. How do they want the wearer to feel?

6. Design a t-shirt for an extreme sport. Include an image and a slogan.

Cliffhangers

Exploring how writers create suspense in stories

Developing a story structure

A cliffhanger is an exciting end to part of a story. It is a moment of drama – as if you are hanging off the edge of a cliff!

Writers use cliffhangers to keep readers in suspense. They make the reader want to read on, quickly.

Read the two cliffhangers on these pages.

Joe Simpson is a mountaineer. He describes a terrible fall. (This is from a true story.)

> … I fell silently, endlessly into nothingness, as if dreaming of falling. I fell fast, faster than thought, and my stomach protested at the swooping speed of it. I swept down, and from far above I saw myself falling and felt nothing. No thoughts, and all fears gone away. So this is it!
>
> From *Touching the Void* by Joe Simpson

Activities

1. Which words from this extract fit into these groups?

   Emptiness   Speed

2. What does Joe mean by the words 'so this is it'?
   a) I'm going to be safe.
   b) I'm going to die.

In this story, a surfer is having problems.

Glossary

reef – a ridge of rock

wetsuit – a rubber suit
worn for water
sports

Suddenly he knew only great tiredness. He was numb to the bone with cold. Even the wetsuit which covered him in a layer of rubber could not keep it out. His hands and feet were blue…The next wave…curled over his head, hung for a moment, then dropped on him with its full weight…Then out of the violent swirl came the reef: Skullcrack!

From *Skullcrack* by Ben Bo

HELP

Think carefully about:
- the **narrator** (who tells the story).You will need to use either 'I' or 'he'.
- the **description** of how the character feels and thinks
- the **plot** – what happens next
- **word choice** – use words that make strong images in the reader's mind.

Activities

3. Why do you think the writer calls the reef Skullcrack?
4. Choose one extract. Write the next paragraph of the story.
5. Plan how the **story** might unfold and end. Make some notes and share your ideas with a partner.

HELP

Remember, a good **story** has:
- a gripping opening
- a clear plot
- a crisis
- a resolution (satisfying ending).

 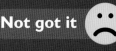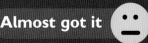

Extreme sports challenge

Complete the Extreme sports challenge. Start at number 1 and work through to number 4.
Good luck!

1 % = per cent

It means 'in every hundred'. 10% means 10 in every 100. It comes from the Latin word *centum* meaning 100.

These words have the same root. Match each one to the right meaning.

century	one hundredth of a metre
centimetre	an insect with many legs
centipede	one hundred years

Find some more words beginning with the root 'cent...'
Use a dictionary if necessary.

2 Adverbs tell us how something happens. They can describe verbs (doing words).
Adverbs often end in –ly, e.g. softly

Work out what these adverbs are. (Clue: look at the stories on the Cliffhanger pages.)

S_le_tly (without noise)

En_less_y (without end)

Su_de_ ly (out of the blue)

3 Connectives can help to put instructions in order.
Choose suitable connectives to finish the instructions below.

Skateboarding tricks: the ollie

_____, put your front foot on the middle of the board and your back foot on the back.
_____, bend your knees.
_____slam your back foot down hard.
At _____, jump in the air and pull up your knees.
_____, as you land, bend your knees.
Roll away!

| Second | Finally | Then | First | the same time |

4 Short sentences and punctuation can make a story exciting.

Edit this story to give it more effect. You could:
- add punctuation, e.g. full stops, exclamation marks, commas
- take out or add a few words
- shorten the sentences.

Will had done many bungee jumps and he had never felt scared before but this time he did and he felt really scared. And then he knew what was wrong and it was that the leg harness did not feel tight and he panicked.

Well done!
You have completed the Extreme sports challenge.

The Black Death

Contents

Introduction

This unit will take you back in time. You will meet a nasty and cruel killer – the Black Death.

Your English skills will help you to:

- work on a shocking news story
- judge a murder case
- imagine what it was like to have the Black Death
- play a dangerous game of death
- look into the famous diary of Samuel Pepys.

Finally, you will use all your English skills to do the Black Death challenge.

Text to share

Sometimes it came by road, passing from village to village, sometimes by river, as in the East Midlands, or by ship, from the Low Countries or from other infected areas... It is very difficult for us to imagine the impact of plague on these small rural communities, where a village might have no more than 400 or 500 inhabitants. Few settlements were totally depopulated, but in most others whole families must have been wiped out, and few can have been spared some loss, since the plague struck at rich and poor alike.

From 'The World Upside Down', by J. Bolton in *Black Death in England*

The year is 1352. A deadly illness has struck Europe. Millions of people are dying.

You have written a news report about it, but your editor has sent it back with a memo and some pictures.

Memo

Good report, but please make a few changes:
1. Check and correct spellings.
2. Add a sub-heading for the third paragraph.
3. Choose a picture to use with the report.
4. Write a caption for the picture.

Your report

Black Death sweeps Europe

A horrible sickness has killed millions of people. The Black Deth – or bubonic plague – causes hedaches, fever and swellings. It is very painful and it is dedly.

The Black Death came to Italy in ships from Asia. It has spread through Italy, France and the rest of Europe. It has spread through Britain too.

We guess there are 75 million people in Europe. The Black Death may have killed one third of the population. That is about 10 million people!

So many people have been killed, there are now not enough people to do all the work.

Check spellings.

Give this paragraph a sub-heading.

Check your maths. Two thirds is 50 million. So what is one third?

Add a picture and caption for it.

HELP
A **sub-heading** divides up text. It tells the reader what the text below is about.

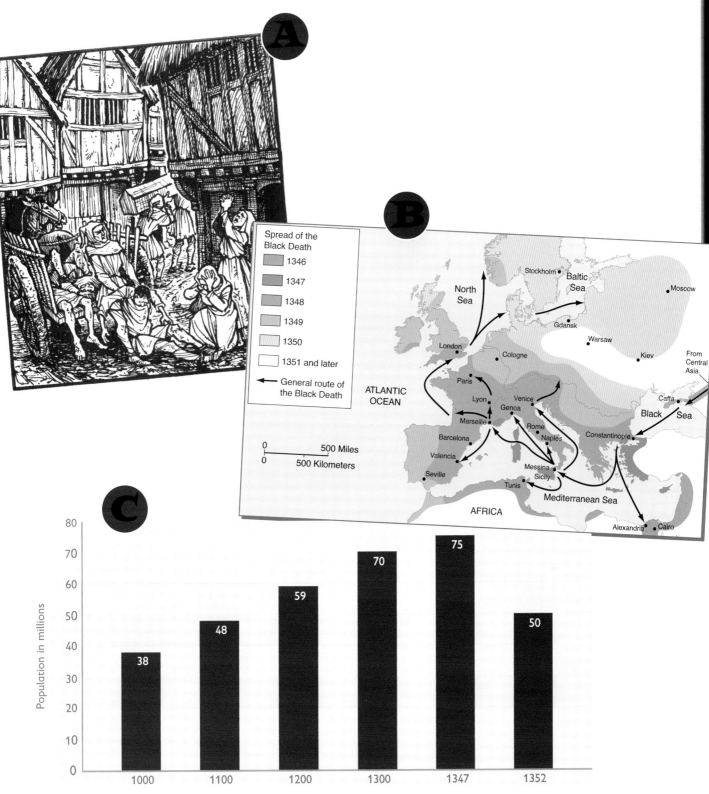

A

B

Spread of the
Black Death
- 1346
- 1347
- 1348
- 1349
- 1350
- 1351 and later
→ General route of
the Black Death

North Sea
ATLANTIC OCEAN
0   500 Miles
0   500 Kilometers
Stockholm • Baltic Sea
Moscow •
Gdansk •
Warsaw •
Kiev •
From Central Asia
London •
Cologne •
Paris •
Lyon •
Venice •
Genoa •
Marseille •
Rome •
Naples •
Caffa •
Black Sea
Constantinople •
Barcelona •
Valencia •
Seville •
Messina •
Sicily •
Tunis •
Mediterranean Sea
AFRICA
Alexandria • Cairo •

C

Population in millions

Year	Population
1000	38
1100	48
1200	59
1300	70
1347	75
1352	50

Activity

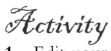

1. Edit your report. Write it out again, making changes that your editor has asked for.

HELP

A **caption** is a phrase or sentence that describes a picture.

Deadly pests

What was most to blame for the Black Death?

You are the judge in this murder case. Here are the three suspects.

I like to live near humans – in and around houses. I travel with humans too. I go around the world in ships.

I'm not feeling well. The Black Death means death for me too.

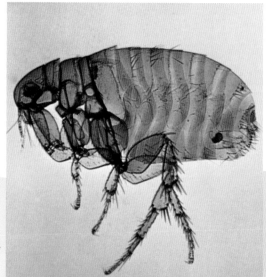

I am a flea. I'm very small – only about 2 mm. I can jump about 200 times my size. Can you work how much that is?

I get around – usually on black rats. But I'm not fussy. Humans will do too. I love warm blood.

The Black Death makes me sick. I drink more and more blood, but keep being sick.

I am a bacterium (germ). I am called Yersinia pestis. I cause the Black Death.

I live in the rat's blood. The flea drinks the blood and sucks me into its stomach. When the flea lands on a human, it is sick and I get into the human.

When I infect a human, there are millions of me in every drop of blood.

I am deadly.

HELP
- You could start your speech by stating 'I believe that…'
- Then list the reasons for your views.
- Try to include some facts as evidence.
- Use persuasive words, e.g. *obviously… surely… it is clear…*
- Finally, sum up your views.

Activities

1. With a partner, talk about each suspect and its part in the spread of the Black Death.
2. Decide which suspect is most to blame. Write a short speech to explain why.

The victim

The Black Death was a name for bubonic plague.

If you have bubonic plague, this is how you suffer:

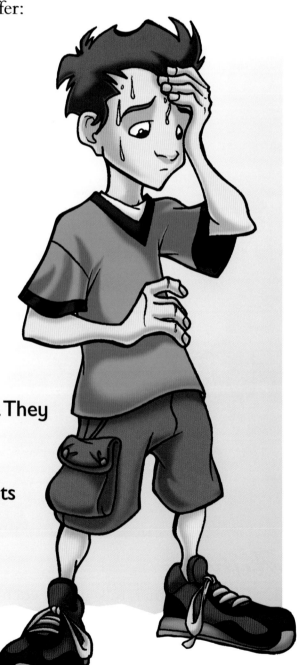

1 You get a headache.

2 You feel cold then hot and sweaty.

3 Your body aches and you feel sick.

4 The flea bites show as rosy red spots.

5 Buboes – big lumps – grow on your neck, under your arms and at the top of your legs.

6 Pus and blood oozes from the buboes. They grow to the size of eggs.

7 Your body bleeds inside and black spots show under the skin.

8 You may die within a week.

There are two other forms of plague you might get:

1 Pneumonic (say *new-mon-ick*) plague

This causes chest pains, coughing up blood and frothy spit. You will probably die.

2 Septicemic (say *sep-ti-see-mick*) plague

The plague attacks the blood. It kills victims quickly.

In 1349, people didn't know how to treat plague. People still get plague today but we can treat it with antibiotics.

Activities

1. Read this nursery rhyme. Can you see the signs of the plague in the words?

> Ring a Ring o' Roses,
> A pocketful of posies,
> Atishoo! Atishoo!
> We all fall down!

2. Imagine you are living in 1352. Write a diary entry. Describe someone who is suffering from bubonic plague.

HELP
Remember that a diary entry can have:
- some recount (what has happened)
- some description (what things look like)
- personal feelings, for example hopes and fears.

Dear diary,

Oh no. Terrible news. Tom has a bad headache...

The Game of Death

You have bought an old box game at a car boot sale. It is called the Game of Death!

Inside the box is:

- a board (see opposite)
- a dice
- four counters.

The instructions (rules) are old and torn. The boy who sold you the game said it was a bit like Snakes and Ladders.

```
Game of Death
Aim:
Number of players:
Instructions:
1. Each player chooses a
2. Take turns
3. Move the same number
4. Read
5. Black spots mean death. If you land
6. The winner is
Remember your best chance of survival is to
stay away from people!
```

Activities

1. Discuss how you think the game should be played.
2. Write out the full set of rules. You can use the old ones to help you, or make up new ones.
3. Test your rules by playing the game.

HELP
Remember, instructions:
- need a **sequence** (order). Use either numbers, letters or words, e.g. *first, next, then*
- often use **imperatives** (commands), e.g. *read, put, move, take*
- should be **short** and **clear**.

68

Rats on ships took plague around the world.

1
You go to live on your own as a hermit.
GO TO BOX 26.

2

3
Your uncle, a sailor, comes to visit.
GO BACK 1 BOX.

4

5
Your neighbour has the Black Death.
MISS A GO.

Pennyroyal is a herb that puts off fleas.

6
You grow pennyroyal in the garden.
GO FORWARD 2 BOXES

7

8

9
You find a dead rat in the kitchen.
GO BACK 1 BOX.

10

Buboes are big swellings – a sign of the plague.

11
One of your family has buboes.
THROW A 4, 5 OR 6 TO SURVIVE.

12

13

14

15
You go to market and see all your friends.
GO BACK 2 BOXES.

16

17
You have a bad headache.
GO BACK 1 BOX.

18
You see a doctor.
THROW AGAIN.

19

20
You are feeling very sick.
MISS A GO.

This was a sign of the deadliest type of plague.

21

22
You go on holiday on your own.
GO FORWARD 4 BOXES.

23

24
You have buboes.
THROW 5 OR 6 TO SURVIVE.

25
Your parents send you to your bedroom for a week.
GO FORWARD 1 BOX.

26

27

28
You have chest pains and cough up blood.
THROW 6 TO SURVIVE.

29

30
Well done! You have survived!

The Great Plague

After 1349, there were many outbreaks of plague. In 1665, it was so bad, that we call it the Great Plague. London was very badly hit.

Hundreds of years had passed since the Black Death, but there was still no cure. Here are some things people did to try to stop the plague spreading.

The Great Plague in London. 1665.

- Everyone, including children, was advised to smoke tobacco.
- Families with plague were locked in their homes for 40 days.
- Searchers were paid to find and bury the dead.
- Dogs and cats were killed.
- Fires were kept burning to clean the air.

Activities

1. Discuss why people may have done these things.
2. Which do you think probably helped most? Put them in order from 1 to 5, with 1 as the best idea. Be prepared to explain your order.

Samuel Pepys lived in London at that time. He wrote about the plague in his diary. Read the extracts below.

The dead must be buried in the day, as the nights are not long enough.

What will be the fashion in wigs after the plague is done, as nobody will dare to buy any hair, for fear it has been cut off the heads of people dead from the plague.

But lord! What a sad time it is to see no boats on the River.

HELP

Think about:
- the numbers of people who died
- people's fears
- why there were no boats on the River Thames.

Activities

3. What do we learn about the Great Plague from Pepys' diary extracts?
4. Imagine you lived at the time of the Great Plague. Design a leaflet, advising people on how to avoid the plague.

HELP

Remember, advice texts:
- may give **instructions**, using commands
- may give a **choice** of suggestions
- will try to **reassure** the reader.
- often use **bullet points**.

Complete the Black Death challenge
Start at number 1 and work through to number 4.
Good luck!

1 Often, we make a plural by adding s, e.g. cat, cats.
Some plurals are irregular – they do not follow the usual pattern.

Here are some irregular words. Write the plural for each one. You may find a dictionary helpful.

child	woman	foot
mouse	bacterium	

List any more irregular plurals that you know.

2 In the words ring o' roses, the o' means 'of'.

We can use an apostrophe to show missing letters.

What are the missing letters in the following words?

I'm	he's
she'll	don't
couldn't	

3 We can use connectives to show why something happens.

Use so or because to complete these sentences:

> a) Rats live near humans _____ they can eat their food and waste.
>
> b) The flea is sick _____ it has bacteria in its stomach.
>
> c) Humans grow ill _____ a flea bites them.

4 Some people want their diaries to be private. Samuel Pepys wrote his diary in code. This made it difficult for anyone else to read.

Here is a diary written in code.

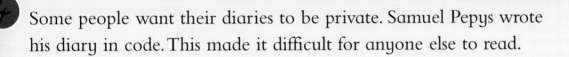

Nmd czx h vhkk qtkd sgd vnqkc!

To decode it, write down the next letter in the alphabet. So where you see a write b, and where you see b write c and so on. (Write a for z.)

a b c d e f g h i j k l m n o p
q r s t u v w x y z

Well done!
You have completed the Black Death challenge.

73

Crime

Contents

Talking about why there are laws
Looking at laws that affect young people

Understanding data about youth crime
Explaining the effects of anti-social behaviour

Comparing reports of crimes past and present

Making decisions, like a magistrate

Completing a poem about prisons
Developing views and arguments about prison

Puzzles on punctuation, the use of slang, bullets points and a slogan.

Introduction

Crime is a danger to everyone. This unit will help you to think about how crime can affect you.

You will use your English skills to:

- test what you know about law
- think about how young you can be to be a criminal
- look back at crime 100 years ago
- judge cases, like a magistrate
- think about the effect and experience of being prison.

Finally, you will use your English skills to complete the Crime challenge.

Text to share

I think that most kids forget they have the power to say 'no' to crime and instead do silly things to impress their friends.
Yaz, 16, Leicester

Crime is committed by kids out of control. I think the parents are to blame.
Lucy, 13, Liverpool

I don't think that we should blame the parents because they can't keep an eye on their children 24 hours a day.
Jac, 11, Carlisle

Children that commit these crimes should be sentenced to tougher punishments and not be tolerated.
Tom, 14, London

The law

- Talking about why there are laws
- Looking at laws that affect young people

Rules help people to do things together. Good rules keep people safe. They try to make things fair.

We use rules in lots of different places and situations.

No Armbands Beyond This Point

Please Shower Before Entering The Pool

Activities

1. Here are some examples of when and where we use rules. Some **vowels** are missing. Work out what they are.

   sch_ _ l
   g _ m _ s
   dr _ v _ ng _ c _ r

2. In each case, what might happen if there were no rules?

3. Where else do we have rules?

HELP

The **vowels** are a, e, i, o u. The other letters of the alphabet are called **consonants**.

76

Laws and crimes

The rules for a country are called laws. They help people to live together. A crime (or offence) is when someone breaks the law.

Look carefully at this picture.

Activities

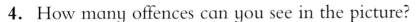

4. How many offences can you see in the picture?

5. Which do you think is the worst offence? Explain why in a sentence. Begin your sentence 'I think … is the worst offence because…'

HELP

Look at:
- parking
- litter
- damaging public property
- zebra crossing
- stealing
- drinking and driving
- dog mess
- drunk and disorderly behaviour.

Laws and young people

Some laws are for young people. Here is a list of things you can do at different ages. The ages are scrambled.

a. You can have a part-time job at **hirtteen**.

b. You can ride a moped of up to 50ccs at **teenxis**.

c. You can open a bank account in your own name at **evens**.

d. You can pilot a plane at **eventseen**.

e. You can have a tattoo at **egihteen**.

f. You can enter a pub, at **urfoteen**, but you can't buy or drink alcohol there until you are older.

Activities

6. Unscramble the ages and write them out, e.g. a. = thirteen.

7. Think of one more law for young people, linked to age. Write it down.

HELP

Think carefully about:
- safety
- ownership
- respect
- public health.

 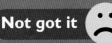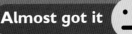

Youth crime

- Understanding data about youth crime
- Explaining the effects of anti-social behaviour

 In the UK, the law says children under the age of 10 cannot be charged with a crime.
In France, the age is 13, and in Spain the age is 16.

HELP

Think about:
- how much children understand about right and wrong at different ages
- the responsibility of parents
- the effect of a criminal record.

Activities

 1. What do you think is the right age? Why?

 Read these facts and figures about youth crime.

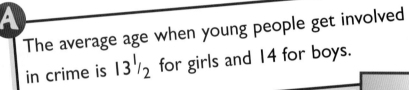

A The average age when young people get involved in crime is $13^1/_2$ for girls and 14 for boys.

B Almost half of all young people admit to having committed a crime at one time or another.

C One in five young people, aged between 10 and 15, has been a victim of crime.

 2. Match the facts to the right graph, e.g. A = …

3. Sketch out the graphs and add some **labels**.

 4. How do graphs help you to understand facts?

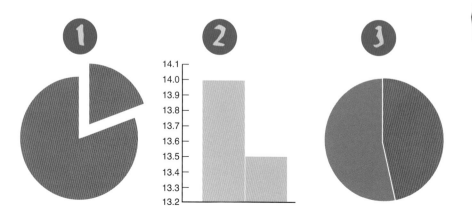

HELP

Some **labels** you could use:
- girls
- boys
- victims of crime
- young people who have committed a crime.

ASBO

New laws have been made to help control youth crime. An ASBO is an Antisocial Behaviour Order. An ASBO can stop someone from going to a particular place or carrying certain things.

Glossary

antisocial behaviour – doing things that are unfriendly or upsetting to others

abusive – rude, aggressive

Activities

5. Look at the types of antisocial behaviour in the grid below.

Type of behaviour	Why it is antisocial
Abusive language	People can find this hurtful or threatening.
Drunken behaviour	
Graffiti	
Litter	
Too much noise	

6. Talk about the effect of each type of behaviour on other people.
7. Copy and complete the grid.
8. Think of two more types of antisocial behaviour.

Crime then and now

Read these four newspaper reports. Two of them are recent. Two were written over 100 years ago.

1

BOY BIRCHED IN VAIN

Arthur Warren, a 12-year-old boy, was charged at Uxbridge with stealing a purse containing £3 16s from another boy in a tramcar.

… [previous] offences included the theft of fruit, rabbits, and a lamp. He had been birched and placed under probation, but without any good results. The lad was sent to a reformatory for five years.

From the *Daily News*

2

Huge rise in mobile phone thefts from children

Up to half a million young people, aged between 11 and 15, fell victim to a mobile phone theft last year... The study also estimates that the overall number of stolen mobiles is more than double the 330,000 officially recorded by the police.

From the *Guardian*

3

Derby Day Charges

At Southwark Police-court, Benjamin Bulfin, 40, … was charged with assaulting Police-constable Grierson … The prisoner said he had been to the Derby and got 'beastly drunk'… Mr. Sheil told the prisoner he had acted like a madman, and sentenced him to a month's imprisonment with hard labour.

From the *Daily News*

4

Bid to cut drink-fuelled violence

Police in Coventry have launched a campaign against drunkenness, violence and antisocial behaviour... Eighty buses are carrying the message in a bid to reduce binge drinking.

From BBC news

our bars are open 24/7

cringe drinking

Glossary

assault – violent attack

binge – having a lot at one time

birched – hit with wood branches

Derby – horse race

probation – supervision by a probation officer

reformatory – place where young offenders were sent to improve their behaviour

HELP

Language is how something is said:
- words
- punctuation
- expression.

HELP

Content is what is said:
- the subject (in these reports, crimes)
- facts
- opinions.

HELP

Think about:
- headlines
- tense (e.g. *past, present, future*)
- facts
- quotations
- opinions
- simple or complex sentences.

Activities

1. Which reports are recent and which are from 100 years ago?

2. Compare the old and new reports. What similarities and differences do you notice in:
   - the **language**?
   - the **content**?

3. Write down three features that all these newspapers reports have.

In court

 Making decisions, like a magistrate

 A youth court is for young people who are in trouble.
There are usually three magistrates in a youth court.

Magistrates:

- are usually unpaid
- listen to the case and make judgements
- have people to advise them on the law.

Read about three cases brought to a youth court, below.

Jon has been smoking weed (cannabis). He thinks cannabis is legal now.

Sol was found in school with a knife in his pocket. He carries it for protection. He's never used it.

Cally had a stolen video phone in her bag. She bought it off her friend for a fiver. She says she didn't know it was stolen.

Legal information

Handling stolen goods

This means selling or keeping something stolen. If you had good reason to know something was stolen, e.g. it was really cheap – you may be found guilty.

Offensive weapons in a public place

It is a crime to carry a weapon in a public place. You don't have to use it to be guilty.

Drug possession

Cannabis is a Class C drug.
You can be fined for having a small amount on you.

Activities

1. Work in pairs or threes. Imagine you are magistrates. Decide whether Jon, Sol and Cally have committed crimes.
2. Use the legal information above to help you.
3. First, talk about your ideas.
4. Then, one of the group should write down the judgements.
5. Use role play to find out more about Jon, Sol and Cally. Take turns to play each character and to answer questions from a magistrate.

HELP
Use this sentence for your judgements:
We believe that ... is guilty/innocent because ....

Words from inside

Read this poem. It is written by someone who has been in prison.

It's humans that they put in prison

It's humans that they put in prison.
It's humans that puts humans in prison.
It's humans that puts humans in prison because
They say they're not humans they're animals.
But I don't know any animals that puts animals in prison.

Eddie S

Activities

1. Eddie compares humans and animals in this poem.
   - What do humans do that animals don't do?
   - What is Eddie saying about humans?
2. Which words does Eddie repeat? Why?
3. Look at the shape and pattern of this poem. As each line gets longer, what happens to the **tone** of the poem?

4. Write an extra line at the beginning of the poem. It needs to fit in with the shape and tone of the poem.

> **HELP**
> The **tone** of a poem is the voice, or mood. It can change to get sadder, funnier, more angry or more serious.

Here, Ryan, a young criminal, talks about coming out of prison.

They think we've changed, but we've not 'cos we've got a lot more money and we're a lot [more] sensible 'cos prison wises you up. 'Cos you meet people in there that's been where we've been, done what we've done, and they've learned from it, and now they're expanding, and then they'll just say to you, 'This is what you should do' and they say, 'When you get out, they give you [a] number and they say phone, we'll sort some business out'. And they're giving us contacts, from Liverpool, Wales, people from other parts of the country. They're giving us contacts, for where we can find bigger and better ways.

From the *Guardian*

Activities

5. What does Ryan learn in prison?
6. Do you think he has changed? If so, how?
7. List three reasons why it is good to send people to prison.
8. List three reasons why is it not good to send people to prison.

HELP

Think about:
- public opinion
- fairness
- punishment
- mixing with other criminals
- other sorts of penalties, e.g. *community service*
- cost of keeping prisoners.

Crime challenge

Complete the Crime challenge.
Start at number 1 and work through to number 4.
Good luck!

1 This text needs proofreading. The **proper nouns** need capital letters. Write out the text, putting in the capital letters.

> There are many stories about detectives. sherlock holmes is a well-known detective. sherlock dresses in a deerstalker hat and cape. He lives in baker street, in london.

> miss marple is a little old lady. She is nosy and clever. hercule poirot is a smart detective. He comes from belgium.

2 Here are some **slang words** to do with crime. Match up the slang with the formal words.

Slang	Formal
porky pies	thief
tea leaf	prison
cop shop	lies
cough up	police station
the nick	confess, own up

3 Bullets points help to organize writing.
Read the advice text, below. Organize it into bullet points.

> Know the IMEI number of your phone. If your phone is stolen, give the IMEI number to the police. To find the IMEI number, dial * # 0 6 #. Keep your phone out of sight in public places.

HELP
A **slogan** is a catchy phrase. Slogans are used in adverts or to summarize ideas.

4 Here is a **slogan**, written like a text message. It reminds people how to keep their mobile phones safe.

Write it out in full.

Lokit, Mrkit, KEPit, Usit, DntLOsit!

Well done!
You have completed the Crime challenge.

Fashion

Contents

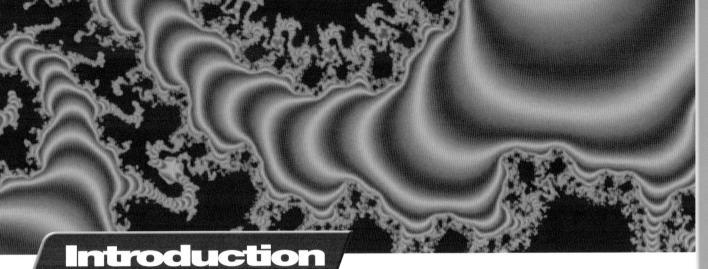

Introduction

Exciting. Glamorous. False. Whatever you think of fashion, it affects everyone – from how you wear your hair, to what you have on your feet.

In this unit, you will use your English skills to explore:

- what fashion is
- how fashions change
- that classic item – jeans
- who the real fashion victims are
- how to be a designer.

Finally, you will use your English skills to complete the Fashion challenge.

Text to share

Why is fashion generally regarded as so unimportant? Clothes are more important, at least initially, than education, where we live, what we drive, how we vote, our religion. I don't mean having the latest thing. I mean as a way of looking at and judging a person; because we all do it. We look for clues that make us think a person is 'all right' (the suit) or possibly 'a threat' (hooded top). When we get to know someone, the clues we get from fashion are not important.

Adapted from an article by Annalisa Barbieri, *The Guardian*

Fashion is...

- Exploring what fashion is all about
- Writing your own thoughts about fashion

📖 Look carefully at the pictures on these pages.

Activity

1. What can you tell about the people from the way they dress?

   Think about:
   - what they might do or be
   - how they want people to treat them
   - what they are saying about themselves.

   Write some **notes** for each picture.

HELP
Notes can be just key words and phrases.

90

Fashion usually means clothes but it can also mean:

hairstyles   music   games   mobiles   furniture

Read these comments about fashion.

Fashion tells us about others.

Fashion is a waste of money.

Fashion is costly.

Fashion makes us all the same.

Fashion is fun.

Fashion is a way to express yourself.

Fashion is a way to link up with others.

 Activities

2. Talk about what you think fashion is.

3. Write a short paragraph about fashion (at least three sentences).

HELP
Choose the comments you agree with, and add your own ideas too.

Fashion over time

 Commenting on how fashion affects us

 Look carefully at this timeline. It shows some changing fashions over the last 500 years.

Elizabethans – high frilly collars

Victorians – bustles puff out the back of skirts

1500   1600   1700   1800

Georgians – large, striking wigs

Activities

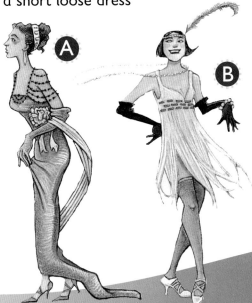

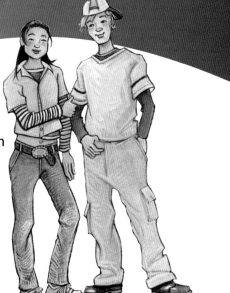

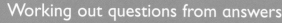

94

Activities

1. Look at pictures A and B. Which one fits the caption?
2. How would these fashions affect the way you live?
3. Write a sentence for each picture. Say what you think the fashion tells us about the people.
4. In your mind, add another 100 years to this timeline. Sketch what you think might be the fashion then. Add the date and a **caption**.

HELP
Think about how these fashions might:
• make you feel
• make you move
• make you behave
• need time and money
• stop you doing some things.

HELP
Start your sentences: I think the … show that these people …

HELP
A **caption** describes a picture.

The 1920s flapper girl, with a short loose dress

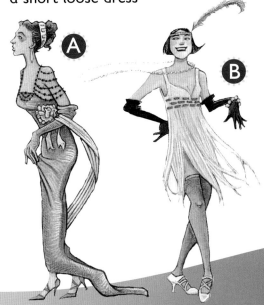

A

B

1900

2000

Modern youth fashion

Blue jeans

Here is the answer sheet for a quiz about jeans. The question sheet has been lost.

Answers

1. Jeans are made from denim – a tough cotton fabric.

2. This is because denim is dyed with indigo.

3. Levi Strauss started to make them in the 1870s as work overalls.

4. They started in America, but now they are worn all over the world.

5. In the 1950s they were made popular by film stars such as James Dean and Marlon Brando.

6. There have been many styles, such as stone-washed, bootcut, baggy and cropped.

HELP
A **question** ends with a question mark. Questions often start with the words: what, why, when, where, who, how.

Activities

1. Look at each answer and talk about what the **question** might be.
2. Write down the list of questions.

Here are some views on jeans. Talk about them with a partner.

You wouldn't catch me wearing them – my dad wears them!

I wish I had invented blue jeans... They have expression, modesty, sex appeal, simplicity.

Yves Saint Laurent

They're comfy – good for messing about in.

My baby sister has little ones – they look so dinky.

HELP

Think about:
• their different styles
• their wide appeal
• their physical toughness.

Anyone can wear jeans. Any age – any place.

I never take mine off – my mum goes mad!

HELP

Write at least three sentences. You can use some of the quotations, but add your own views too.

Activities

3. Will jeans always be popular?
4. Write a paragraph giving your views on jeans.

Fashion victims

Are you a fashion victim? Some people only buy certain brands of clothing. They only shop in particular shops.

As a country, we spend a lot of money on clothes and footwear. Look carefully at the data below.

Article II. Spending on clothing and footwear in the UK, 2004

Clothing	£37 billion
Footwear	£6 billion
Total	£43 billion

Average weekly spending on clothes and footwear (2002-2004) in the UK.

£5.30 — Girls, aged 13–15

£2.50 — Boys, aged 13–15

Activities

1. Are these statements true or false (look at the data)?
    - In the UK, we spend more on shoes than clothes.
    TRUE /FALSE
    - Girls aged 13 to15 spend more than twice as much on clothes and footwear as boys.
    TRUE/FALSE

2. Interview a partner to find out if they are a fashion victim. Write down six questions.

HELP
Here are some questions to start with:
- Is fashion important to you?
- Do you have a favourite brand/shop?
- Do you have clothes that you do not wear because they are not fashionable?

Fashion is a global industry. Clothes sold in Britain are made all over the world. This provides jobs in other countries, but sometimes the working conditions are poor.

 Read the story of Mara from Cambodia.

Mara's Story

- I start work at 7.30 am.
- I sew trousers all day.
- My target is 120 pairs of trousers an hour.
- I earn 75p an hour.
- In a normal day, I have to sew 960 pairs.
- Overtime starts at 4 pm.
- I'm not allowed to take a break.
- Sometimes we don't stop until 8 pm.

Adapted from Oxfam website

Activities

3. Talk about Mara's day. Note the main points.

4. Write an entry for Mara's diary. Explain what happens and how she feels.

 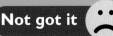

Wild designer

Research, plan, create and present your own fashion designs

You are going to be a fashion designer.

Your task:

Design a **fashion accessory** based on wildlife.

 1

Choose your accessory:

bag	belt
hat	jewellery
scarf	wallet

2

Choose the wildlife, e.g. insects, plants, birds.

3

Study the colours, patterns and shapes in your wildlife. Make sketches and **notes**.

HELP
Notes can be just words or phrases.

 Plan wildlife designs for your accessory. Try out different ideas.

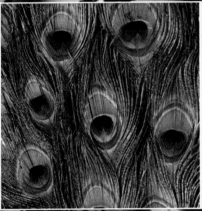

 Present your final design neatly on paper. **Label** your design. Explain your choices and decisions.

HELP
Labels explain the detail of a drawing or diagram.

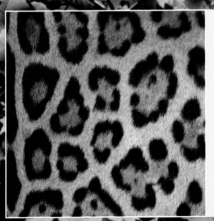

 Present your ideas to your partner, group, or class.

LOOK BACK   Not got it 😞   Almost got it 😐   Got it 😊

Fashion challenge

Complete the Fashion challenge.
Start at number 1 and work through to number 4.
Good luck!

1 Homophones are words which sound the same, but have different spellings and meanings. For example:

jeans = denim trousers

genes = part of a living cell.

Find the homophones in the letter string, below. Explain their meanings.

blueblewwaistwastewriterightsunsonhereheardeardeer

2 Asking questions is a skill. We can ask them in many ways.

Closed questions look for one answer, e.g. What colour is the sky?

Open questions look for wider information, e.g. How would you describe the sky?

Here are three topics. Write a closed and an open question about each topic.

1. jeans
2. hairstyles
3. a fashion designer

3 Writing down part of what someone says or writes is called a quotation.

These quotations are too long. Make them shorter by picking out the important parts. Remember to use quotation marks.

> **a** "Fashion makes us all the same. Don't you think? I do."
>
> **b** "What's the most important thing in fashion? Well it can only be one thing. Colour is everything in fashion."
>
> **c** "I don't know much about fashion. I really don't. But one thing is clear: fashion rules the lives of everyone."

4 Fashion is often about **opinion**. Read this review of a fashion show. List all the opinions you can find.

HELP
Opinion is what someone thinks. In contrast, a fact is true and can be proved.

Josh Jolly is a fantastic fashion designer. He has worked in London, Paris and Stoke. This was his third fashion show, and the best so far.

All his dresses were about bubbles. The bubble-wrap dress was stunning. The model had a big shiny bubble hat on – a very clever idea.

However, the best dress was the bubble-gum ball gown. It was in a pretty pink shade. The skirt blew big pink bubbles as the model walked down the catwalk. It was bubble magic!

Well done!
You have completed the Fashion challenge.

Fantasy worlds

Contents

Introduction

Writers can take us to exciting new worlds – worlds where anything can happen.

In this unit you will use your English skills to explore:

- worlds of the imagination
- characters that live in fantasy worlds
- places where they live
- stories that they have to tell
- a quest of your own.

Finally, you will use your English skills to complete the Fantasy worlds challenge.

Text to share

What type of character are you? A hero with a brave heart and a will to do good? A warrior with the power to fight off evil monsters? An undiscovered expert in magic and spells? Or perhaps you are a traveller in a secret world, beyond the reach of most of us on Earth.

If this is where your mind likes to be, then you belong to the world of fantasy – a magical world of adventure where the impossible can and does happen!

Imaginary worlds

- Working out the ingredients of a fantasy story
- Developing a fantasy story through talk and role play

Fantasy means something imaginary or strange. Fantasy stories take the reader to new worlds, where strange things happen.

secalp wen

cigam   **live**   **regnad**

elpoep egnarts   **tseuq a**

serutaerc

Glossary

a quest – a search for something

Fantasy Story

 Activity

1. Look at the picture above. The words are ingredients for a fantasy story. Work out what they are.

HELP

Re-order the letters. Write the last one first, etc.

104

Here is part of a fantasy story:

> It was a smooth red candle. Joe lit it. The flame glowed like a small bead. Then it fizzed, and the flame grew strong and bright. For a long time, Joe stared at it, the flame growing brighter and brighter. It was dazzling. He looked away and gasped. His bedroom had gone. He was now sitting in a strange place...

 ## Activities

2. Think of a way to continue the story. Describe where Joe is now sitting, e.g. a dark, damp cave; an empty room full of cobwebs; a wooden cabin on a sailing ship.

3. What do you think the magic has come from?

4. What do you think will happen to Joe?

5. Prepare a short improvisation to show what might happen next.

HELP

Think about
- what Joe might feel
- how he might look
- what he might say
- what he might do.

Characters

- Looking at character types
- Creating character game cards

In fantasy stories, there are lots of types of character. These can include aliens, wizards and warriors.

The 'hero' of a fantasy story may be an ordinary boy or girl. The hero is a 'goody' and he or she has to fight a 'baddy'.

The hero may have:

special skills   **good qualities**   **a friend to help**

a weakness   **an enemy**   **a problem**

Glossary

armour – covering to protect the body in fighting

character – a person in a story

Activities

1. Match the characters and descriptions.

Character	Description
giant	a small being with magical powers
wizard	a being from another planet or world
knight	a woman who uses magic
witch	a creature like a huge man
fairy	a fighter, who has a horse and armour
alien	a man who uses magic

2. Write down the names of three **fantasy stories** you know.

3. Choose four different characters from your named fantasy stories. What types of character are they?

HELP

Fantasy stories can be

- books
- films
- games
- TV series.

Look at these game cards. They are based on characters from a fantasy story. The characters have marks out of 10 for some qualities.

What can you tell about them?

Joe Lando

Type:	Boy
Age:	13
Height:	1.46m
Bravery:	5
Magic:	0
Fighting skill:	3
Speed:	5
Honesty:	7

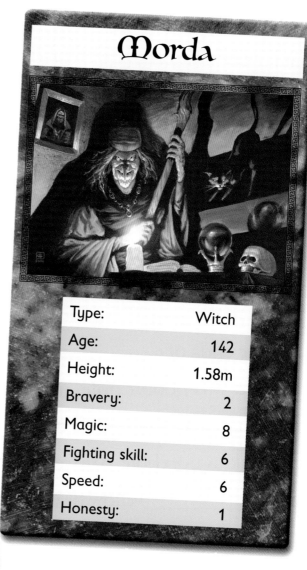

Morda

Type:	Witch
Age:	142
Height:	1.58m
Bravery:	2
Magic:	8
Fighting skill:	6
Speed:	6
Honesty:	1

Activities

4. Think of three characters for a fantasy story:
    - a hero (male or female)
    - a hero's friend
    - a baddy.
5. Design a game card for each character.

HELP

Don't forget to:
- list qualities you want, e.g. *kindness, loyalty, humour, strength*
- give them marks out of 10
- draw a picture.

 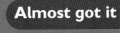

A fantasy writer needs to tell a reader about where the story happens. This is called the setting.

Read the text below. It describes where a creature called a hobbit lives. Fill in the gaps, using the words in the box.

> In a _____ in the ground there lived a hobbit. Not a nasty, _____ wet hole, filled with the ends of _____ and an oozy smell... it was hobbit hole, and that means comfort. It has a perfectly _____ door like a porthole, painted green, with a _____ yellow brass knob in the exact middle.
>
> From *The Hobbit* by J.R.R. Tolkien

dirty
shiny   worms
hole   round

HELP

To **imply** means to suggest something without actually saying it. What do these words suggest:
- 'comfort'
- 'perfectly round'
- 'exact middle'
- 'shiny yellow door knob'

Activities

1. Copy out the text and write in the missing words.
2. What does the text tell us about where hobbits live?

3. What does the text **imply** about hobbits?

A **fantasy story** can be set in many different places, e.g. palaces, ships, islands, forests, etc. The writer has to imagine the setting in their mind, then describe it to the reader.

Look carefully at the pictures on this page.

HELP

Fantasy stories can be:
* set in the future, or an alien place
* a quest for individuals
* set in the countryside or mountains
* linked to a magic place, or element, e.g. *water*
* a battle between kingdoms.

Activities

4. Each picture could be a setting for a different fantasy story. What sort of story do you think would suit each setting?

5. Choose one picture. Describe the setting in your own words, as if it is the beginning of a fantasy story.

The story

Most good stories follow a pattern. It is like climbing a hill. There are four stages:

1. opening
2. development
3. climax
4. ending.

Look at the diagram below. It explains what happens at each stage.

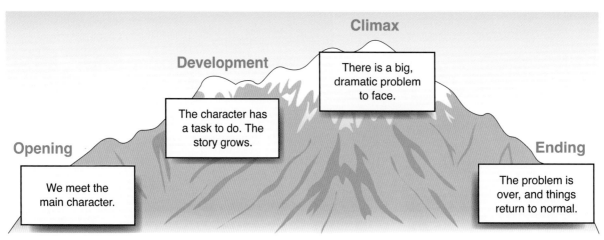

Climax

There is a big, dramatic problem to face.

Development

The character has a task to do. The story grows.

Opening

We meet the main character.

Ending

The problem is over, and things return to normal.

Activities

1. Which is the most exciting part of a story?
2. Which is the longest part of a story?
3. In which part does the writer need to catch the reader's interest?
4. Think of a story. It could be a book or film. Copy and complete the grid below.

Stage	Storyline
Opening	
Development	
Climax	
Ending	

Write an outline of what happens in the story at each stage.

110

Good stories have a mix of dialogue and narrative.

Read the two texts below.

Glossary

dialogue (say *die-a-log*) – characters talking
narrative – the descriptions and action

A

'Give me the candle,' said Morda.
'No,' said Joe.
'If you don't, I will die.'
'Like all the others you killed!'
'They were fools!'

HELP

Think about these questions:
• Which is most exciting?
• Which gives most detail?
• Which helps you 'see' the scene best?

B

'Give me the candle,' said Morda. She held out five skinny white fingers.
Joe knew it was a trick.
'No,' he said.
She took a step closer. Joe took a step back – toward the cliff edge.
'If you don't, I will die.' Her voice was thin and weak.
Joe laughed.
'Like all the others you killed!' He would not be tricked again.
'They were fools!' hissed the witch.

HELP

When writing **dialogue**, remember:
• to use speech marks
• to put punctuation inside the speech marks
• to say exactly what the character says.

 Activities

5. Which text do you think works best? Why?
6. Write what happens next. Use some **dialogue** and some narrative.

The quest

Planning your own fantasy story

Activity

Plan your own story set in a fantasy world.
Imagine you are a hero, on a **quest**.

- Follow the path and the instructions.
- Write notes for each stage.

HELP

A **quest** is a search for something

1 Introduce your hero and the quest.

2 Your hero meets a friend or helper. Describe him or her.

HELP

Choose one quest:
- to find the Jewel of Truth
- to find the potion of everlasting life
- to find the rightful king or queen.

HELP

Choose one helper:
- Merla the elf
- Tiz the robot
- Lex the wizard.

3 Think of an object that will help your hero. It could be powerful or magical. Describe it.

4 Go on a journey. Describe the place you travel to. How does it make your hero feel?

5 You come across an evil creature. Describe it and what happens.

6 One of you is hurt. Describe what happens.

7 The climax. This is the most exciting part of the story. Describe what happens.

8 The end. Describe how things work out. Has the quest been successful?

HELP

Choose one journey:
- down a river
- up to a castle tower
- on a horse or other creature.

HELP

Choose one climax
- there is a fight
- there is a test
- there is great danger.

 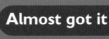

Fantasy worlds challenge

Complete the Fantasy worlds challenge. Start at number 1 and work through to number 4.
Good luck!

1 Write down as many words as you can, using letters in the word.

fantasy

2 In the dialogue below, the **speech marks** are missing. Write it out, putting the speech marks in place.

Hi, said Joe. The girl did not say anything.
I'm Joe. What's your name? asked Joe.
Steffi, she said.
Nice to meet you, Steffi.

HELP

Speech marks are at the beginning and end of what a character says.

3 In the text below, the bold words are in the present tense. Change them to the **past tense**.

Steffi **looks** around. Water ran down the slimy walls. Cobwebs **blow** about in the empty windows. Then she saw a pair of eyes glowing in the shadows. They **are** like nothing she **has** ever seen. She **shivers**.

HELP

We usually tell stories in the **past tense**, e.g. *he walked* and not *he walks*.

4 Here is the jumbled outline of a story.

Match each description to the right stage.

Stage	Description
Introduction	Joe and Steffi find her father and return home happy. Joe has to return to his own world.
Development	Morda finds out and traps Joe. The candle will give her extra powers. Trying to kill Joe, she slips and falls to her death.
Climax	Joe buys an odd red candle from a junk shop.
Ending	When the candle is lit, it takes him to a land ruled by the evil witch, Morda. He meets Steffi. Her father has been taken to the witch's cliff top castle. They go to free him.

Well done!
You have completed the Fantasy worlds challenge.

Funny ha ha

Contents

Introduction

Do you like a good joke? Are you ticklish or a bit of a clown?

This unit will help you use English skills to:

- explore why we laugh
- think about clowning around
- enjoy some silly rhymes
- have fun with performing a poem
- share your best jokes.

Finally, you will use your English skills to do the Funny ha ha challenge

Text to share

Address www.people.howstuffworks.com/laughter.htm

Human beings love to laugh, and the average adult laughs 17 times a day. Humans love to laugh so much that there are actually industries built around laughter. Jokes, sitcoms and comedians are all designed to get us laughing, because laughing feels good. For us it seems so natural, but the funny thing is that humans are one of the only species that laughs. Laughter is a great thing – that's why we've all heard the saying, 'Laughter is the best medicine.' There is strong evidence that laughter can actually improve health and help fight disease.

From www.people.howstuffworks.com

Having a laugh

- Talking about what makes us laugh
- Describing laughter

What makes us laugh?

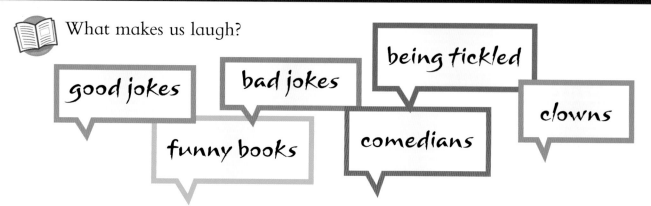

good jokes

bad jokes

being tickled

funny books

comedians

clowns

Read the text below. Fill the gaps with words from
the box.

| giggle | relax | medicine |
| happy | body | |

Laughing shows we are _____ and amused.
There are many ways to laugh. For example, we can
chuckle or _____ .

Laughter is catching. One person laughing can make
someone else laugh. It helps us to _____ and to mix
with others.

Laughter tells the _____ to make endorphins (say
en-door-fins). These make us feel good. So laughter
can be the best _____ .

Activity

1. What makes you laugh? Tell a partner and give an
   example.

HELP

For example: 'I laugh at
the TV show... It's really
funny when...'.

Different types of laughter

We each laugh in a different way. We sometimes use **similes** to describe laughter:

- He laughed like a train.
- He sniggered like a machine gun.

Some people believe that other animals laugh. Chimpanzees make noises that could be laughter when chasing or being tickled. Rats 'chirp' when tickled.

Glossary

A **simile** compares one thing with another, using the words 'like' or 'as…as'.

For example: 'She's as strong as a horse', 'They ran like the wind'.

Activities

2. Think of someone you know well. Describe the sound of his or her laugh. Use a simile.

3. Describe the face of someone laughing. What happens to the lips, cheeks and eyes?

4. Think of an animal that makes sounds like laughter.

Funny people

Some people earn a living by making us laugh, e.g. comedians such as Dawn French, presenters such as Ant and Dec, and actors such as Will Smith.

Someone who does silly things to make people laugh is often called a clown. Clowns have been around for a long time. In the middle ages they were known as jesters. Shakespeare had jesters in some of his plays.

Nowadays, many clowns look similar. There is a list of the features of a clown, hidden in this word ring.

Activity

1. List the features of a clown, hidden in the word ring.

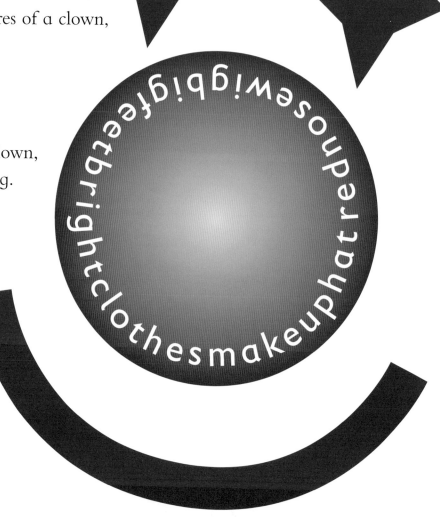

Clown eggs

Every working clown has a different face design. In
Britain, a record of every design is kept – on an egg!

Activities

2. Draw a simple clown face design.
3. Give a partner step-by-step **instructions** to draw
   your design. (Do not let them see it.)
4. How clear were your instructions? How carefully did
   your partner listen? (You can tell by how similar your
   designs are!)
5. Write an **acrostic poem** about clowns.

Funny rhymes

Working out what makes some poems funny

 Read these three poems.

A

I am writing these poems
From inside a lion,
And it's rather dark in here.
So please excuse the handwriting
Which may not be too clear.
But this afternoon by the lion's cage
I'm afraid I got too near.
And I'm writing these lines
From inside a lion,
And it's rather dark in here.

by Shel Silverstein

B

There was young lady of Twickenham,
Whose boots were too tight to walk quickenham;
She bore them a while,
But at last, at a stile,
She pulled them both off and was sickenham.

by Mal Peet

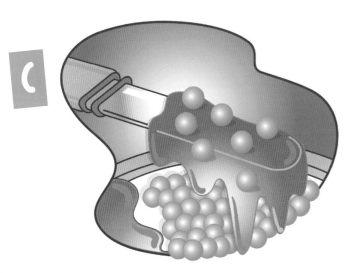

I eat my peas with honey;
I've done it all my life.
It makes the peas taste funny,
But it keeps them on the knife.

ANON

Poetry explorer

1. Choose a poem.
2. Use this explorer (a flow chart) to work out what makes it funny.

Do you understand it?
— Yes
— No

Read it again. Ask a partner or teacher for his or her ideas.

Does it have words that rhyme?
— Yes
— No

Which are the best rhymes?

What has made this poem funny?

Why does the poet use them?

Is there a rhythm to the poem?
— Yes
— No

Are there any silly ideas?
— No
— Yes

Clap out the rhythm

Are there any made-up, funny or rude words?
— No
— Yes

Why does the poet use them?

Glossary

rhyme – a similar sound in the endings of words

rhythm – a pattern of beats

Funny creatures

 Performing a poem
 Writing an information text

Read this poem.

Phinniphin

by *Frank Collymore*

The tide is in,
The tide is in,
The Phinniphin
Are out.

They love the sea,
The salty sea,
Of this there is no
doubt.

O watch them flop
And slip and slop
With clumsy hop
Right past

The sandy beach
Until they reach
The friendly sea
At last.

But when the tide,
The shifty tide
Stays right outside
The bar,

They can't go in
The Phinniphin;
The Phinniphin
Cannot go in:
They'd have to hop
Too far.

Glossary

bar – a sandbank

124

Activities

1. Prepare a dramatic reading of this poem with a partner or group.

    Think about:
    ● who will read what
    ● how the words will be read
    ● actions
    ● sound effects.

2. Perform your poem. Afterwards, talk about what went well and what you could improve.

3. Create a page on Phinniphin for an **information book**.

    Imagine:
    ● what the phinniphin look like
    ● the sounds they make
    ● how they move
    ● what they eat.

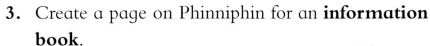

> **HELP**
>
> Remember, an **information book** can have:
> • sub-headings
> • text in paragraphs
> • pictures
> • diagrams with labels.

Tell us another...

Everyone enjoys a good joke.

A Doctor, doctor, everyone thinks I'm a liar.

I can't believe that!

B How do chickens dance?

Chick to chick.

C Knock, knock.
Who's there?
Boo.
Boo who?
Don't cry. It's only a knock, knock joke!

D How can you tell an elephant's been in your fridge?

There are footprints in the butter.

Many jokes use puns.

Q: Why did the mushroom go to the disco?
A: Because he was a fun guy.

In this joke, the pun is on the words 'fun guy', which sound like 'fungi'. All mushrooms are fungi.

Q: Why did the apple go out with the pineapple?
A: Because it couldn't find a date.

Here the play is on the word 'date'.

Glossary
pun – a pun is a play on words, using one word sounding the same as another.

Activities

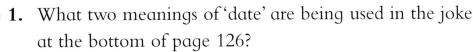
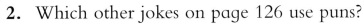

1. What two meanings of 'date' are being used in the joke at the bottom of page 126?
2. Which other jokes on page 126 use puns?
3. Explain how they work.
4. Think of another joke that has a pun. Tell it to a partner.

Funny descriptions

When people have a car accident, they have to write down what happened. Sometimes the **descriptions** sound funny, if they haven't used words carefully. Here are some descriptions that people wrote on car insurance claim forms.

> The pedestrian did not know where to go, so I ran over him.

> I crashed into a parked lorry coming the other way.

> The car in front stopped at the traffic lights, so I had no choice but to hit him.

HELP

The **descriptions** should be clear and make sense.
For example:
'The pedestrian did not know which way to go. He stopped in the middle of the road. I slammed on my brakes, but I couldn't stop the car in time, so I ran over him.'

Activities

5. What makes these descriptions sound funny?
6. Rewrite the descriptions so that they sound right.

Funny ha ha challenge

Complete the Funny ha ha challenge. Start at number 1 and work through to number 4. Good luck!

1 A joke with no punctuation is no joke!
Copy the joke below. Add the right **punctuation** to the end of each line.

> Knock knock
> Who's there
> Robin
> Robin who
> Robin you, so give us all your money

2 Count up the **syllables** in each line of this limerick.

> There was an old man with a beard
> Who said it is just as I feared
> Two owls and a hen
> Four larks and a wren
> Have all built their nests in my beard.

In most limericks, lines 1, 2, and 5 have the same number of syllables. Lines 3 and 4 have fewer.

3

Q: **What is the difference between a tree and a train?**

A: **One sheds its leaves, and the other leaves its shed.**

This joke works by using a word as both a **noun** and a **verb**.
The noun shed = a building.
The verb sheds = loses.

What other word in the joke is both a noun and a verb?
Give the meaning for both the verb and the noun.

> **HELP**
> A **noun** is a naming word.
> A **verb** is a doing word.

4 Here are some **similes**.

> Her tummy felt like jelly.
> He was as silly as wiggly string.

> **HELP**
> A **simile** compares one thing to another. It uses the words 'like' or 'as…as'.

Finish off these similes:
- The sea was like…
- The puppy was like…
- The lesson was as boring as…

Well done!
You have completed the Funny ha ha challenge.

Deserts

Contents

Introduction

Deserts are some of the wildest places on Earth. They are full of dangers: heat, dryness and deadly creatures.

In this unit, you will use your English skills to:

- find out where deserts are in the world
- explore the beauty of sand dunes
- find out about the world's largest desert: the Sahara
- learn how to survive in a desert
- meet some deadly desert creatures.

Finally, you will use your English skills to do the Desert challenge.

Text to share

Proverbs and sayings about deserts and camels:

All sunshine makes a desert.

Any water in the desert will do.

As the sands of the desert are to the wary traveller, so are words to he who loveth silence.

If the camel gets his nose in a tent, his body will soon follow.

A camel never sees his own hump, but that of his brother's is always before his eyes.

Deserts of the world

Deserts are amazing places. They can be really hot, and they can be really cold. Europe is the only continent with no desert.

This world map shows some of the largest deserts.

NORTH AMERICA

Mojave Desert

SOUTH AMERICA

Atacama Desert

Key
◻ Desert

Patagonian Desert

Activity

1. In this list, the deserts have lost some letters:

   _ t _ c _ m _   N _ mib

   Moj _ ve   S _ h _ r _

   _ r _ bi _ n

Check the map above and write out the names in full.

HELP
Remember that a place name begins with a capital letter.

132

📖 Did you know…

A desert is a place which has less than 250 millimetres of rain per year.

Deserts can be scorching. Temperatures can be over 50°C in the Sahara.

Antarctica is a sort of desert. In some parts it never rains.

Deserts can be freezing. Winter in the Gobi Desert can mean temperatures of -20°C.

Some deserts are sandy. Some are huge salty plains. Most deserts are stony or rocky.

Activities

2. Write a sentence for each desert, saying which continent it is in, e.g. The Atacama Desert is in South America.

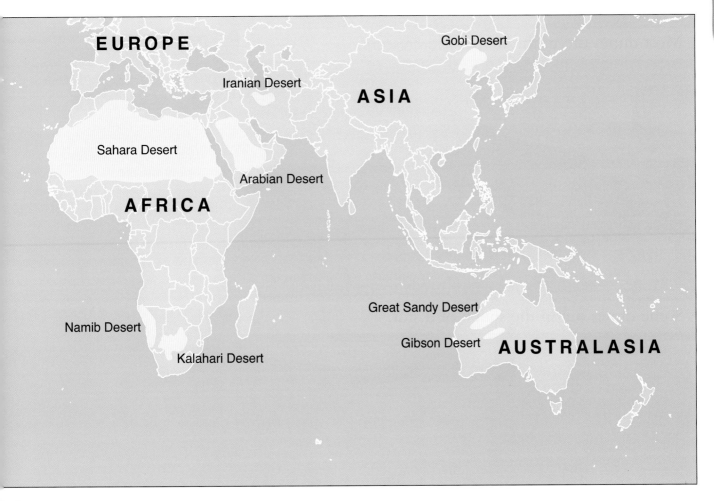

3. Draw a KWL grid. Fill in what you can now, and add more as you work through the unit.

What I already **know**	What I **want** to know	What I have **learned**

Sand dunes

Exploring sand dunes with shape poems

Many deserts have sand dunes. Look at the sand dunes on this page. The wind blows the sand around. The sand makes patterns and shapes.

Most dunes are in the shape of a crescent.

Glossary

dune – a mound of loose sand shaped by the wind

Glossary

crescent – a narrow curved shape, like a new moon

Some dunes are in the shape of a star.

Some dunes are in the shape of ripples.

134

Shape poems

Bigger than the last.

Another dune appears

Just when I think I'm at the top

movingalwaysmoving

hotsand hotsand hotsand

alwaysmoving alwaysmoving

hotsand hotsand hotsand

Activities

1. Look at the shape of Poem 1. How does the shape echo the meaning?

2. Look at Poem 2. How does the shape and colour echo the meaning?

3. Write a shape poem about sand dunes. Make your words follow the shape or pattern of a sand dune.

HELP

Here are some words you could use in your poem:

bank bend blows
burning curves deep
golden heat hill
mound rise sand
scorching shifts soft
sweep warm yellow

Sahara

 Understanding data
Writing complex sentences

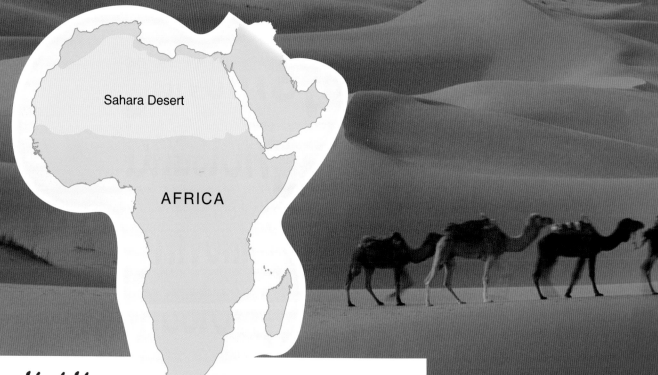

The Sahara, in Africa, is the largest desert in the world. It is as big as the USA.

Many countries are part of the Sahara.

Sahara Desert

AFRICA

Activities

1. How much of Africa is covered by the Sahara? Is it:
   - 3/4
   - 9/10
   - 1/3

2. One quarter of the Sahara is sand dunes. One quarter is the same as:
   - 10 %
   - 25 %
   - 75 %

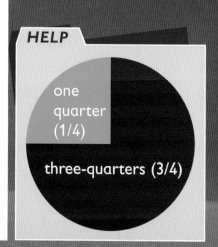

HELP

one quarter (1/4)

three-quarters (3/4)

Read the hot facts about the Sahara.

🌴 The Sahara is very dry. It gets less than 8 cm of rain a year.

🌴 Dust storms can blow for days. They cover everything in sand.

🌴 The highest temperature ever recorded was in the Sahara. It was 58 ºC.

🌴 Nomadic people live in the Sahara. They travel from place to place.

🌴 Some people run marathons in the Sahara. The races are up to 250 km!

🌴 Another race in the Sahara is the Dakar race. It is with motor vehicles.

HELP

A **simple sentence** has just one clause, e.g. *I got wet.*
A **complex sentence** has two clauses, e.g. *I got wet because it was raining.*
A **connective** joins clauses in a complex sentence, e.g. *I got wet because it was raining.*
Some other connectives are: so, which, until.

 ## Activity

3. Each 'hot fact' is made up of two **simple sentences**. Join them together, to make one **complex sentence**. You can use a **connective** or change the wording.

Read this page from a survival handbook.

Glossary

sandstorm – winds full of sand

survival – staying alive

THE SURVIVAL HANDBOOK

Tips for desert survival

You must have water to live. Be aware of how much water you have. Look for sources of water.

Heat and sunlight will make you need more water. Try to find shelter in the day. Shelter in the shade of rocks or bushes.

Sweating is the main way to lose water. Travel at night. You will sweat less and lose less water.

Drink water regularly. If the temperature is over 38°C, drink one litre of water per hour.

Sandstorms are a danger. Protect your face. Mark the way you are going. Then lie down and wait for it to pass.

Activities

1. Could you survive in the desert? Try the survival quiz, below. You will find all the answers in the Survival Handbook opposite.

2. Write your own question about survival in a desert.

HELP

Your own question could be about sandstorms. Remember that all questions end with a question mark.

Survival quiz

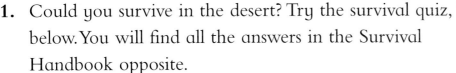

1. What you need most is
   - food
   - water
   - toilet paper

2. Try to find shelter
   - from the hot sun
   - from animals
   - from homework

3. What is the main way to lose water?
   - talking
   - sweating
   - drinking

4. It is best to travel
   - after breakfast
   - at night
   - in the day

5. When the temperature is over 38°C
   - drink 1 litre of water per day
   - drink 1 litre of water per hour
   - drink 1 litre of water per minute

Snakes and spiders

 The desert is a dangerous place. It is home to some dangerous creatures.

Do you know what this spider is called? Start at the centre of the web and spell out her name.

FACT BOX

- She has strong venom.
- Her bite will not usually kill, because of the small amount of venom.
- The male spider is not poisonous.
- This spider spins some of the strongest web silk.

Snakes

Snakes are another creature of the desert. Read this poem about a rattlesnake.

Still as stone
Skin like dead grass
Its eyes, slits in the sun.
Rattlesnake waits.

Forked black tongue
Slips out
Tastes the scent.

Rattlesnake waits.

Mouse stops.
Something's wrong.
Mouse blinks.

Rattlesnake strikes.

Activities

1. The poem doesn't have a title. What could the title be?
2. There are 33 words in this poem.
   - How many have the letter 's' in them?
   - How many begin and end with an 's'?
   - How do all these words with 's' in them help the meaning of the poem?

3. Write some more lines to add to the end of this poem.

HELP

- What exactly happens to the mouse?
- Add another verse of three lines
- Use just 2 or 3 words per line
- Use the 's' sound wherever you can.

 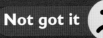

Desert challenge

Complete the Desert challenge
Start at number 1 and work through to number 4.
Good luck!

1 A thesaurus lists synonyms (words with a similar meaning). Here are some words to go in a thesaurus. Decide whether they go under the heading HOT or COLD.

| warm | freezing | icy | boiling | scorching | chilly |
| baking | burning | cool | red-hot | sub-zero | bitter |

2 A hyphen can join two words together to make a new word, e.g. blue-black.

Use hyphens to join some of these words. Make three new colours to describe the desert.

| red | yellow | silver | gold | grey |
| pink | orange | ginger | amber | |

3

Alliteration means repeating the same sound at the beginning of words, e.g. sea of sand.

Here are some descriptions. Add another word to each one, using alliteration.

- The snake s_____ across the sand.

- The w _____ winds whipped up the sand.

- The desert was dry and d_____ .

4

Write these sentences, adding a **connective** to link the clauses.

- A camel's thick coat protects it from cold a_ _ keeps out the strong heat from the sun.

- Camels store water in their stomachs s_ they can go days without drinking.

- A camel can live off fat wh _ _ _ it stores in its hump.

HELP
Some **connectives** are: because, although, so, and, but, while.

Well done!
You have completed the Desert challenge.

OXFORD
UNIVERSITY PRESS

Great Clarendon Street, Oxford OX2 6DP

Oxford University Press is a department of the University of Oxford.
It furthers the University's objective of excellence in research,
scholarship, and education by publishing worldwide in

Oxford   New York

Auckland   Cape Town   Dar es Salaam   Hong Kong   Karachi
Kuala Lumpur   Madrid   Melbourne   Mexico City   Nairobi
New Delhi   Shanghai   Taipei   Toronto

With offices in

Argentina   Austria   Brazil   Chile   Czech Republic   France   Greece
Guatemala   Hungary   Italy   Japan   Poland   Portugal   Singapore
South Korea   Switzerland   Thailand   Turkey   Ukraine   Vietnam

Oxford is a registered trade mark of Oxford University Press
in the UK and in certain other countries

British Library Cataloguing in Publication Data

Data available

ISBN-13: 978-0-19-832552-9

10 9 8 7 6 5 4 3 2 1

Printed in Thailand by Imago.

ACKNOWLEDGEMENTS

We are grateful for permission to reprint the following copyright material:

BBC article 'Bid to cut drink-fueled violence', reprinted from BBC News at
bbcnews.co.uk, by permission of the BBC.

J Bolton: extract from 'The World Upside Down' in *Black Death in England*
edited by Mark Ormrod and Phillip Lindley (Paul Watkins, 1996), reprinted
by permission of the publisher.

British Library extracts from *Daily News*, 'Boy Birched in Vain', 27.11.1918
and 'Derby Day Charges', 28.05.1886, reprinted by permission of the
British Library.

Frank Collymore: 'Phinniphin', copyright © The Estate of Frank
Collymore 1994, first published in *A Caribbean Dozen* edited by John Agard
and Grace Nichols (Walker Books, 1994), reprinted by permission of the
Collymore Estate.

The Guardian headlines following the Asian Tsunami, copyright ©
Guardian Newspapers Ltd 2004, used by permission of GNL; 'Millions lack
food and shelter', *Guardian Unlimited*, 27.12.04; Patrick Barkham: 'Boy, two,
found by aunt on the Internet', *The Guardian*, 29.12.04; Patrick Barkham
and Jackie Dent: 'Tourists return after holiday nightmare', *The Guardian*,
28.12.04; Jason Burke: 'Smashed hotel reveals its dead', *The Guardian*,
29.12.04; Alok Jha: 'Out of the blue, a deadly wall of water', *The Guardian*,
27.12.04; Sam Jones: 'One mother's choice...which child to save', *The
Guardian*, 31.12.04; and Mark Tran: 'Please help. Give us aid', *Guardian
Unlimited*, 31.12.04, reprinted by permission of GNL.

Donal MacIntyre: extract from transcript of talks with two teenage drug
dealers, *The Guardian* 13.7.05, copyright © Guardian Newspapers Ltd 2005,
reprinted by permission of GNL.

Metropolitan Police Service: mobile phone theft campaign slogan used
by permission of MPS.

Oxfam: 'Mara's story' adapted from 'Mara's Day' on
www.oxfam.org.uk/coolplanet/teachers, reprinted by permission of Oxfam
GB, Oxfam House, John Smith Drive, Cowley, Oxford OX4 2JY, UK. Oxfam
GB does not necessarily endorse any text or activities that accompany the
material nor has it approved the adapted text.

Julia Pearson: 'I am the Wind' first published in *New English First* by
Rhodri Jones (Heinemann Education, 1988).

Tim Radford: extract from 'Deadly monsters in the air spawned by
nature', *The Guardian*, 5.5.99, copyright © Guardian Newspapers Ltd 1999,
reprinted by permission of GNL.

Eddie S: 'It's humans that they put in prison' from *The Man Inside: an
anthology of writing and conversational comment by men in prison* edited by Tom
Parker (Michael Joseph, 1973).

Shel Silverstein: 'It's Dark in Here' from *Where the Sidewalk Ends* (Jonathan
Cape, 1984), copyright © 1974, renewed 2002 Evil Eye, LLC, reprinted by
permission of Edite Kroll Literary Agency Inc.

J R R Tolkien: extract from *The Hobbit* (HarperCollins, 2004), copyright J R
R Tolkien 1937, reprinted by permission of HarperCollins Publishers Ltd.

Alan Travis: extracts from 'Huge rise in mobile phone thefts from
children', *The Guardian*, 8.1.02, copyright © Guardian Newspapers Ltd 2002,
reprinted by permission of GNL.

We have tried to trace and contact all copyright holders before publication.
If notified, the publishers will be pleased to rectify any errors or omissions
at the earliest opportunity.

P4/5 Photodisc/Oxford University Press; **p6/7** Photodisc/Oxford University
Press; **p8** Photodisc/Oxford University Press; **p9** Photodisc/Oxford
University Press; **p10r&l** NASA/Oxford University Press; **p10tm**
Stockbyte/Oxford University Press; **p10bm** Hemera/Oxford University
Press; **p11l** Norbert Shaefer/Corbis; **p11m** Renault UK; **p11r**
Photodisc/Oxford University Press; **p12** NASA/Roger Ressmayer/Corbis; **p14**
MovieStore; **p15** Bruce Weaver/AP/Empics; **p16/17** Photodisc/Oxford
University Press; **p18/19** Photodisc/Oxford University Press; **p21** Getty
Images; **p23** Photodisc/Oxford University Press; **p25** Dimas Ardian/Getty
Images; **p26** Photonica/Getty Images; **p27** Morris L Manning/AP/Empics;
p28 Shropshire Star; **p10** NASA/Oxford University Press; **p31**
Photodisc/Oxford University Press; **p32/33** Photodisc/Oxford University
Press; **p42/42** Digital Vision/Oxford University Press; **p44/45** Digital
Vision/Oxford University Press; **p46/47** Photodisc/Oxford University Press;
p48l G Lepp/Corbis; **p48mb** C McLennan/Empics; **p48mt** Buzz Pictures;
p48tr Photodisc/Oxford University Press; **p48br** P Winter/Corbis; **p50** Buzz
Pictures; **p51l** David Sanger/Alamy Images; **p51r** Photodisc/Oxford
University Press; **p52** F Ostrop/Empics; **p53** F Ostrop/Empics; **p54** Digital
Vision/Oxford University Press; **p57** Digital Vision./Oxford University Press;
p58/59 Photodisc/Oxford University Press; **p61r** Corbis/Digital
Vision/Oxford University Press; **p61l** Digital Vision/Oxford University Press;
p64l Tom McHugh/Science Photo Library; **p64r** Science Source/Science
Photo Library; **p65** NIAID/CDC/Science Photo Library; **p68** Michael
Taylor/Oxford University Press; **p70** Mary Evans Picture Library; **p71** Mary
Evans Picture Library; **p72/73** Digital Vision/Oxford University Press;
p74/75 Photodisc/Oxford University Press; **p76l** Rebecca Naden/PA/Empics;
p76r Martin Sookias/Oxford University Press; **p79** Bob
Watkins/Photofusion Picture Library/Alamy Images; **p80** Hulton
Archive/Getty Images; **p81t** West Midlands Police Authority; **p81b** John
Martin/Alamy Images; **p83** Photodisc/Oxford University Press; **p84** Paul
Doyle/Alamy Images; **p85** Jiri Rezac/Alamy Images; **p86/87**
Photodisc/Oxford University Press; **p88/89** Corel/Oxford University Press;
p90l Getty Images; **p90b** ImageSource/Oxford University Press; **p90tr**
Photodisc/Oxford University Press; **p94/95** Michael Taylor/Oxford
University Press; **p95** S Hammid/zefa/Corbis; **p97** Tong Chhin Sothy/Getty
Images; **p98/99** Photodisc/Oxford University Press; **p100/101** Corel/Oxford
University Press; **p102/103** Corbis/ Digital Stock/Oxford University Press;
p105 Photodisc/Oxford University Press; **p109bl** Corel/Oxford University
Press; **p109tl&r** Corbis/Digital Stock/Oxford University Press; **p114/115**
Corbis/Digital Stock/Oxford University Press; **p116/117** Ingram/Oxford
University Press; **p119** Bettmann/Corbis; **p121tl&b** Ingram/Oxford
University Press; **p121tr** Tony Eldridge/Clowns-International; **p128/129**
Ingram/Oxford University Press; **p130/131** Photodisc/Oxford University
Press; **p134t** Photodisc/Oxford University Press; **p134b** Peter
Carsten/National Geographic Image Collection; **p136/137** BL Images
Ltd/Alamy Images; **p140** Dr Gary D Gaugler/Phototake Inc/Alamy Images;
p141 Robert E Barber/Alamy Images; **p142/143** Photodisc/Oxford
University Press.

Illustrations are by Richard Anderson: **p39**; Martin Aston: **p40**; Barking
Dog: **pp13, 37, 63, 69, 77, 78, 96, 110, 132/133, 136**; Milivoj Cevan:
p107; Martin Cottam: **p62**; John Hallett: **pp123, 126**; Peter Lubach:
pp36, 67, 104; Chris Molan: **p124/125**; Pulsar: **pp66, 82**; David Semple:
p41; Tom Sperling: **pp92, 93, 112/113, 138**.